The Conservative Gene

How Genetics Shape the Complex Morality

of Conservatives

The Conservative Gene

How Genetics Shape the Complex Morality
of Conservatives

Michael C. Anderson

SBPC

SIMMS BOOKS PUBLISHING CORPORATION

SBPC

SIMMS BOOKS PUBLISHING CORP.

Publishers Since 2012

Published by Simms Books Publishing Corporation

Jonesboro, GA

Library of Congress Cataloging in Publication Data

2021906421

The Conservative Gene

How Genetics Shape the Complex Morality of Conservatives

ISBN: 978-0-9996882-3-6

Printed in the United States of America

Book Arrangement by Simms Books Publishing

Editor Mary Hoekstra

Cover by Michael C. Anderson

Dedication

To my wife Eva who is a constant source of inspiration.

Acknowledgement

I wish to thank Mary Hoekstra, my tireless and ruthless editor. She challenged me to be the best.

James Simms, my publisher, for his interest and support.

William F. Buckley, for building the foundation for a Conservative Ideology.

R. Emmett Tyrell, for explaining the Conservative mind.

John Jost, for his studies of the psychology of Conservatives.

TABLE OF CONTENTS

PREFACE

In the preface to my first book, *The Progressive Gene: How Genetics Influence the Morality of the Left* (2017), I said that the book had written itself. I was driven by concerns over the state of affairs in American politics and wanted to try to understand the sources of the tribalism that has infected our society. Specifically, I was trying to understand the thinking of Left-wing Progressives and their fanatical efforts to eradicate inequality in the United States.

The Progressive Gene was stimulated by the research of Jonathan Haidt, who identified a set of genetic moral foundations that influence human behavior. Haidt showed those moral foundations were distributed across the political spectrum, leading to variations in the ways different groups view the moral principles that drive the public vision of government. Haidt's research showed those on the Left are driven by a morality focused on Caring and Fairness. Those on the Right are driven by different moral foundations, including Loyalty, Authority, Sanctity and Liberty.

My first book discussed the development of Progressivism and how morality shaped its political ideology throughout history. My conclusion was that the Progressives' zeal for the disadvantaged made them blind to the difficulty of fixing inequality. They have tried many solutions to the problem, starting with the creation of Utopian communities in the 19th Century. For a hundred years, Progressives thought Socialism was the answer, until it was shown to be corrupt, unequal, and dysfunctional. Then, starting in the 1960s, the

Left became focused on fixing Capitalism by changing it into a collectivist engine. The problem with that approach was, and is, that big government cannot deliver on fixing society's ills. Its inefficiency and waste prevent the achievement of Progressives' dreams.

It occurred to me, early in my research for *The Progressive Gene,* that I should write a companion book about Conservatives, turning my attention from the political Left to the political Right. This approach made sense for two reasons. First, Jonathan Haidt had described the entire political spectrum, both Left and Right, so the data were already available. Second, I wanted to explore the Right side of the political spectrum to see specifically how it differed from the Left.

As an academic, I wanted the research to take me where it must, separate from any preconceived notions I may have had. I consider myself a political moderate, which means I support positions most would consider both Left and Right. Like many people, I tend to be more liberal on social issues and conservative on economic ones. Anyone who observes the Right knows it is open to criticism, just like the Left. The Left agitates for improvement, while the Right tries to keep the Left from being too ambitious.

After completing half of *The Conservative Gene*, I paused. I was intellectually and personally drawn to examine the tribalism that began and continues to haunt our country. I had to try to understand tribalism, and then write about it. Where had this tribalism come from and what impact will it have on the future of our political system? Out of that activity came my second book, *Tribalism: The Curse of 21ˢᵗ Century America* (2019), which addresses issues that have driven the Right and the Left farther apart over the last 25 years.

I realized again that this divisiveness can be traced back to moral foundations. The political morality of the Left and Right are considerably different now, so it is more difficult for them to compromise. In the past, compromise was possible because there were moderates in each party who acted as communication links and worked to bring opposing views together. Those moderates have retired now, and the ones who remain are more extreme. Each of the parties has become fragmented by ideological elements and can no longer achieve agreement even among themselves.

After publishing *Tribalism*, I returned to the topic herein. *The Conservative Gene: How Genetics Shape the Complex Morality of Conservatives* explains how moral decision-making on the Right differs from that process on the Left. Conservatives do not have the same passion Progressives do. Why? What makes the Right seem so passive? Why does the Right take criticism without defending itself?

American political behavior is driven by the momentum created by those on the Left, who want to fix all social problems. Those on the Right typically oppose change and react against it almost reflexively. Behavior that is reactive is suspect when it does not offer a better alternative. What do Conservatives offer that brings value to politics in 21ˢᵗ

Century America? If you look at Conservatism throughout history, you can see an evolving process. From the time man appeared on earth until the Enlightenment in the 17th Century, Conservatism was biological, meaning its moral foundations influenced the behavior of conservative people. Conservatives were careful and avoided complex decision making. They were not risk takers. As human history advanced, traditions became an important part of human society, creating links to those aspects of the past that man chose to carry forward. Traditions were always more important to Conservatives than to Liberals because they fit better with Conservative moral foundations.

The first threads of conservative politics emerged in the Tory movement during the Restoration period after King Charles II of England came to power in 1660. A battle began among British politicians over the role of tradition in shaping the path of government. One group, the Tories, took a traditional approach to government that limited the rights of the common man. The opposing group, the Whigs, wanted to put the common man on equal footing with the monarchy and the nobility.

The Glorious Revolution of 1688 produced a new British Constitution and mandated equality across England. The traditionalist Tories fell out of favor until they agreed to accept the rights of the common people. Those same Tories later became the Conservative Party, which sought to protect the traditions of England against the Socialist and Labor parties.

In the United States, during the Colonial period, Americans were divided between Tories, who supported the Crown, and those who advocated a separation from England. After the Constitution was enacted and the American government began to operate, the Federal Government was controlled by a faction known as the Federalists. Not yet a party, they were men who wanted America to resemble the Roman Republic with its strong central government.

The Federalists, under the leadership of Alexander Hamilton, became the Conservatives who valued tradition above a free democracy. The opposing faction, controlled by Thomas Jefferson, favored a strong democracy with power distributed to the states and the people. This fundamental disagreement between Hamilton and Jefferson led to the formation of the first political parties.

Throughout the 19th Century and half of the 20th, Conservatism was expressed as a defense of the status quo and tradition. The formation of the Republican Party, as a reaction against slavery, brought conservatives into politics for the first time.

The Conservative ideology as it exists today first appeared in the United States in the 1950s. It emerged when traditionalists, Libertarians, and Anti-Communists united against their common enemy, the New Deal Liberals, who advocated for change, sought expansion of the welfare state, and were soft on Communism. Later, the Conservative ideology would expand when Neoconservatives and the Religious Right joined the movement.

After the Reagan years, the Conservative Movement fractured and lost its way. Republicans had become enamored with the intellectual shallowness of politics and tried to move forward without an ideology. Conservatives have never been able to build a legitimate response to the cultural changes promoted by the Left. By refusing the debate, they have forfeited their ability to have a say in the government's response to changes in American society.

Today the Conservative Movement is trying to redefine itself to fit the 21st Century, a time beset with tribal conflict. The Right has demonstrated neither the willingness nor the energy to take on the Left, which controls academia and the mainstream media. Conservatives, however, need to aggressively exert their traditional role in human society to check the excesses of the Left and try to bring the country back to the political center. Our country cannot prosper when political engagement is dominated by one side and that side promotes ideas that don't represent a consensus about the path forward.

CHAPTER ONE

INTRODUCTION

*The meaning of conservatism is not that it impedes
movement forward and upward, but that it impedes
movement backwards and downwards—
to chaotic darkness and the return to a primitive state.*

Nikolai Berdyaev

The election of Donald Trump in 2016 drove the level of
polarization and divisiveness in the United States into the
stratosphere. Partisan conflict had been growing over the
previous three decades, aided by the Left-leaning media and
burgeoning 24-hour news cycle. At present, it has reached a
new level where each side sits behind a wall of ideology that
completely blocks compromise. Over the last decade, the
new media darlings, Facebook© and Twitter©, have
exacerbated the problem by amplifying the most extreme
rhetoric from each end of the political spectrum. Through
these conduits, the most vocal receive a disproportionate
share of the microphone, making it appear they represent the
opinions of the majority of the American people. Further
evidence of this divide is the COVID pandemic, which one
would expect to be a uniting force. Instead, it has become
just one more partisan issue.

From the point of view of the Left, Trump's personality is composed of despicable qualities: he is a businessman who is a strong capitalist, a populist who has a sense of the political currents of the country, a man who appeals to groups outside the Progressive milieu, and an out-spoken, irreverent opponent to anyone who criticizes him. Because the Left is used to taking on timid Republicans who don't respond, it drives them crazy to face an adversary who pushes back.

Trump's victory was one of the greatest examples of Democrat miscalculation in the history of the Republic. Putting all their focus on his personality and mocking him as a caricature without substance, the Democratic Party ignored constituencies they normally rely on to win elections. Those same constituencies put the larger-than-life businessman over the top. Trump fully represented the maxim that the results of elections in a democracy are the truth. That is to say, the results of elections are neither accidents resulting from some magical process, nor the votes of an unknown constituency. The simple answer is: Trump understood better than his opponents what the electorate wanted in a candidate, and became a champion of those constituencies. Trump was a populist with an ego; he believed he could succeed at anything, including fixing the major problems in America. He was never a party ideologue, so the Republicans couldn't control him. He talked directly to his constituents to avoid the media bias and shunned lobbyists and PACs. These factors made the Trump administration a jarring ride for traditional Conservative power groups.

After the 2016 election, the Left began to mimic Trump as reactionary, stubborn, and full of invective. Their reaction accelerated the already-apparent ideological polarization in America. Today, Americans won't discuss politics outside the family because the subject is kryptonite. The Left, driven by their fanatical desire to influence social change, seeks to limit the Right's free speech. Their allies, academia and the print and broadcast media, have now been supplemented by the social media as arbiters of the truth. At the same time, the Right is whipsawed between Trump's behavior and their own factionalism.

The polarization in American society has also spilled over into Congress. After six years of Republicans blocking the Obama agenda, the process has been reversed. Democrats have employed their own "rope-a-dope" strategy by which they patiently allow Republicans to wear themselves out with pointless punches so the Democrats can close the debate or argument with fresh jabs and upper cuts.

Can our country afford many more years of government paralysis? As the Federal Government sits idle, significant problems remain and get worse. Healthcare is imploding over the failed Obamacare system with no ultimate solution in sight. Entitlements continue to drain the federal budget on their way to bankrupting the country. While Congress sits idle, the president moved forward via executive order. Trump has been attacked as an authoritarian bully, even though a factionalized, uncooperative Congress is the real problem.

America is moving toward an oligarchy in which a few people and their lackeys control the direction of Congress. Money flows from the elite class through lobbyists, who in turn pull the strings of their politician marionettes. The result is a Congress that has ceased to represent the interests of the American people.

The Left and Right behave differently because each is programmed with a different morality. Moral behavior is partly determined by genetics, resulting in a spectrum of political beliefs. On that spectrum and between the extremes of Left and Right are the moderates, who form a large block unmoved by ideology. The media largely ignore them in favor of the extremes, whose behavior generates greater controversy. Sound bites and ink produce more ad revenue for them.

This book focuses on one of these combatants, the Conservatives, and the goal herein is to examine their biological, psychological, social, and political behavior now and throughout history.

Conservatism

Conservatism is a political and social philosophy that promotes traditional institutions as a foundation for maintaining a stable culture and civilization. Conservatives assert that changes to society must be tempered against tradition in order to maintain stability. Most people see Conservatives as protectors of institutions such as religion, family, and traditional family values, but Conservatives also advocate for small government and property rights.

There is no single set of policies universally regarded as conservative because the application of Conservatism depends on what is considered traditional at any given place and time. Conservatives from different parts of the world—each upholding their own respective traditions—may disagree on a wide range of issues. According to Quintin Hogg, chairman of the British Conservative Party in 1959, "Conservatism is not so much a philosophy as an attitude, a constant force, performing a timeless function in the development of a free society, and corresponding to a deep and permanent requirement of human nature itself."[1] Some have criticized Conservatism as the defense of social inequality and glorification of the elite. Even if this view is correct, it is not intended to harm or exclude those in need of help. It expresses the practical realization that it is impossible and unattainable to build a society based on equality. One need only look at the failure of Socialism to verify the validity of this argument.

Recent data have bolstered the argument that Capitalism, a fundamental component of the ideology of Conservatives, helps all people in society by lowering prices for goods, developing new technologies, and providing services for people. In 1981, 40% of the world's population lived in poverty. In 2020, the number is 10%.[2] These changes have occurred because Capitalism is having more influence around the globe.

The importance of Conservatism in our culture is beyond

---

[1] Hogg, "The Conservative Case." 1959.
[2] Povcalnet, "Poverty Head Count 1981-2030."

debate; it serves to put a brake on the excesses of Progressive action, stabilizing the operations of the Federal Government and protecting traditions human beings generally find sacred and comforting. When the balance between Left and Right breaks down, and Progressives begin to dominate, changes to the system happen more rapidly. The result is instability and tribalism. Progressives always seek to dominate the cultural narrative because that is their nature. They speak loudly for the things they believe. Conservatives seldom speak loudly, unless their beliefs are under imminent threat.

Origins of Conservatism

Conservative thought has been an evolving human characteristic since man appeared on earth. It began as a biological trait, a genetically driven desire to avoid change, a Conservative Gene. Then, at some point, humans began to create traditions that were often based on religion, but also on elements of the human experience that were celebrated and valued. The Conservative Gene was at work, inculcating the veneration of traditions to become a part of the Conservative framework, adding to their foundational, biological Conservatism.

Until the Enlightenment, conservative people had no ideology and no defined political role in government. Still, they tried to apply a brake on progress so that society could move forward in an orderly manner. In Rome it was the conservative Senate against the liberal Assembly. During the Renaissance Period, it was the Catholic Church against Martin Luther. During the Enlightenment, it was the conservative monarchies against Liberalism. In each of these cases, the conservatives represented the status quo, opposed to any faction or belief system that was pushing too hard for change.

During the Enlightenment, the seeds were planted for conservatives to become political. The Conservative Gene energized them to apply their genetic traits to the structure of evolving political systems. They sought ways to use conservative thinking and traditions to guide society forward. In Britain, the Tory Party developed after the Restoration in 1660. Initially the Tories rejected sovereignty by the people and the authority of Parliament, holding to a historical monarchist line. When the Glorious Revolution occurred in 1688 and a new English Bill of Rights came into being, the Tories saw their power ripped away by the expanding rights of the common people. To retain legitimacy, they reinvented themselves by accepting Parliament as the real power in the British Government. Even with this pivot, however, the Tories were marginalized in British politics for 70 years, before they were able to regain their popularity.

One hundred years after the Glorious Revolution, a member of Parliament, Edmund Burke (1729-1797) took a stand against the Enlightenment, and in doing so, gave the word "conservative" its first definition. Burke argued for the value of tradition as a foundation for determining how a society should move forward. In his view, tradition provided a reference frame to keep the rate of societal change under control. Burke was adamantly opposed to the French Revolution and viewed it as an attempt to wipe the slate clean rather than using traditions as a guide for measuring reasonable progress. Burke defended the common-sense approach of the Glorious Revolution as a safer strategy. He employed his conservative beliefs. and the terror in France to remind the British people of what they had achieved and the need for them to stay on the path they had taken.

Conservatism in Germany and France
Germans rejected the Enlightenment because they saw it as a wholesale attack on tradition and God. They refused to accept the concept of "God the engineer" as a replacement for "God the benevolent father." The Germans blamed the French Revolution on the Enlightenment, which they said led to the rise of Napoleon, the wars he caused, and the French occupation of German land.

In 1848, Republican sentiment led to revolts across Europe. In Germany, fear of the revolutionary reaction drove its rulers to give in to public demands for freedom. Then, when that revolutionary fervor subsided, those same leaders took back that power and reverted to the old monarchical systems.

Otto Von Bismarck (1815-1898) came to power in 1862 as Minister President of Prussia. He pursued the goal of uniting the German nation, using a program of revolutionary Conservatism as a state building strategy. Bismarck began the construction of a welfare state that would appease the masses and, at the same time, short-circuit revolutionary tendencies. His approach was designed to satisfy the goals of the Socialist unions within a larger power framework that limited their influence. To his credit, Bismarck's use of a

Conservative ideology succeeded at slowly increasing the rights of the German people.

The French Revolution was a uniquely different story. It caused enormous pain to the French people and affected the politics of Europe for generations. The circumstances driving the French revolutionary forces to tear down their entire society became a lesson about the importance of relying on tradition as a basis for change. It also served as a case study for the value of conservative institutions as a framework for moving a society forward. When all institutions in France were swept away, including the church, the aristocracy, the government, and the sacred traditions, there was nothing left to prevent anarchy. Initial attempts at building a new government failed because there was no consensus on how to govern. Separate groups had their own agendas and would not compromise.

When the French government got on firmer footing in 1796 after seven years of mayhem, it devolved quickly into a dictatorship under Napoleon. His empire lasted until 1815, when the enemies of France forced a restoration of the monarchy. In the next 55 years, France gyrated from republic, to empire, to monarchy and back again; each iteration involving a competition between and among factions for control of the government. The French political system finally stabilized in 1870 when a balanced democracy emerged.

During the years following the revolution, the Conservative Party repeatedly attempted to restore the monarchy, but their efforts failed. The Enlightenment had taken hold, once and for all, so there was no going back to traditional government forms. French Conservatives tried to focus their efforts on tradition, but there was no longer any continuity with the world that had existed before.

Conservatism in the United States
In Colonial America, the first Conservatives were supporters of the Crown, standing against independence. They opposed the Enlightenment Liberalism of the colonists who wanted to break from tradition. Later, after the Constitution was adopted and the American government was in operation, political factions emerged. Disagreements between these groups were based on opposing ideologies. The Federalists, led by Alexander Hamilton, believed the new nation could only survive with a strong Federal Government designed to control the people. He also believed it was the role of the Federal Government to support and foster the growing American economy. Hamilton's opponents, led by Thomas Jefferson, believed strong state governments executing the will of the people was a better model for government. There was no conservative tradition at that time, and one would not emerge until enough time had passed to establish a true American history.

John Adams is often called the most important Conservative of the Colonial period. He believed political tradition had shown the importance of aristocrats in government. Wealthy, well-educated men could be trusted to apply reason to the operation of government, while middle- or lower-class men would rather sell their votes for monetary gain. Adams observed the French Revolution and felt it validated his concerns about discarding tradition in favor of something totally new. To him, the French Revolution showed how a quixotic search for equality had cheated millions out of their lives and property. He believed that men were different, had different ways of pursuing success, and that inequality in human society was inevitable.

Abraham Lincoln (1809-1865) was the most important American Conservative of the 19th Century, participating in the birth of the Republican Party at the time when slavery was threatening to tear the country apart. The party was formed out of the residue of the defunct Whig Party and disaffected Democrats, who didn't agree with their party's support of slavery. The party creation was the expression of a need to guard the tradition of the American Constitution against those who would tear the republic apart. Lincoln brought these groups together in an effort to defend the union against the possibility of Civil War, providing the initial connection between conservative thinkers and American politics.

In the period after the Civil War, Conservatives were driven by their morality, traditions, and their connection to Republican politics. Although the Republican party was formed to oppose the expansion of slavery to the Western territories, it was forced to deal with prosecuting the war and then reconstructing the South. After hostilities ended, Conservatives began to examine American traditions and determine how they might apply to American politics.

In 1870, at the beginning of the Gilded Age, America experienced an excess of both wealth and poverty, Conservatives became part of the growing Progressive Movement that aimed at ending the corruption and exploitation of American workers. Later, in the New Deal years, Conservatives fought to protect the Constitution against changes they feared would turn the American government into an authoritarian state.

After World War II the germ of a Conservative ideology began to develop, broadening the reach of the Conservative Gene. The wellspring for that action was the book, *The Road to Serfdom*, written in 1944 by economist Friedrich Hayek (1899-1992). Hayek's position, based on observing the Soviet Union and Nazi Germany, was that collectivism bred tyranny. Hayek was a Liberal in the classical sense, not the modern American definition. His position, which would later be rebranded as Libertarianism, joined Traditionalism as foundations for a new Conservative ideology.

During the same period, a third foundation appeared; Anti-Communism. Many liberal intellectuals, writing in the post-WWII period, believed Communists had infiltrated the American government and had caused it to adopt a soft approach toward the Soviet Union. The leaders of this group, themselves former Communists, had become disenchanted with Communism as an ideology and wanted to move in a different direction. They saw mid-20th Century Conservatism as a haven for their views.

The watershed for Conservative ideology occurred in 1955 when William F. Buckley began publication of *The National Review*. Through his influence and hard work, Buckley almost single-handedly built a sustainable Conservative ideology. He brought intellectuals together who analyzed and published papers about the theory of Conservatism, and he united the three Conservative factions into one ideology. Traditionalism, Libertarianism, and Anti-Communism became the intellectual framework of Conservativism.

Despite the embarrassing loss of Barry Goldwater in the 1964 presidential election, Conservatives continued to expand their new ideology. In 1973, the Neoconservatives appeared as a new ideological partner. Neocon intellectuals, including Irving Kristol (1920-2009), rebelled against the extreme positions of the new Left during the 1960s and against the McGovern Democrats in the early 1970s. The Neocons provided additional intellectual power to the Conservative movement and helped set the stage for the election of Ronald Reagan. In the late 1970s, the Conservative coalition expanded once again, when the Religious Right joined it.

The Reagan presidency provided a powerful base for the Conservative ideology, but by the end of Reagan's time, its intellectual effort began to wane. The Republican Party had become more focused on winning elections than maintaining ideological rigor.

The George W. Bush years were troublesome for Conservative ideologues because Bush did not follow the

Conservative line. The damage caused by the Iraq War and the recession of 2007 set the stage for the Republican defeat in 2008. By the time Barack Obama was elected, the Republican Party was factionalized and unable to build a unifying message. Donald Trump was elected in 2016 as a populist, rejecting the value of a Conservative label. Trump didn't respond to Republican ideological pressure because he didn't need party money. Today, Conservatives remain on the losing side of the social-ideological battle, even when they have control of Congress and the presidency. Why is this happening?

In succeeding chapters, as you will learn, Conservatives have had a natural aversion to engagement in politics. They do not relish battle, while those on the Left do. Conservative attitudes about American society operate at the gut level, making it difficult for them to articulate an ideology. Not that they care about ideology anyway. Most Conservatives are content living their lives and are not interested in combat.

Format of this book
Chapter 1: Introduction and background for the topics to be discussed in the book.

Chapter 2: Human Evolution and Morality, describes genetic human behavior, including the influence of genetics on morality. It also explains Biological Conservatism and how brain function contributes to a conservative point of view. Lastly, it describes functional differences between the brains of those on the political Left and those on the political Right.

Chapter 3: The Complex Conservative Morality, describes the moral foundations of Conservatives and how those foundations complicate their decision-making. Conservatives must reconcile different moral attributes in order to make moral decisions.

Chapter 4: Conservatism Before the Enlightenment, discusses conservative views prior to 1650. During the period from the beginning of the human species to the Enlightenment, Conservatism was expressed only as a biological trait and a desire to maintain tradition.

Chapter 5: Conservatism Becomes Political, traces the advent of a Conservative political movement in England during the time before the French Revolution. The most well-known Conservative during that period was Edmund Burke, a member of the British Parliament, who developed a philosophy based on the value of tradition as a counterforce against radical political action. Included also are descriptions of English politics from Burke to the present day, along with the history of Conservativism in Germany.

Chapter 6: The American Conservative Movement to 1955, covers American Conservatism before the advent of its ideology. The Colonial period, the presidency of Andrew Jackson, and the Civil War all included expressions of the conservative mindset.

Chapter 7: The American Conservative Movement 1955-1980, marks the period of maturity of a Conservative political ideology. Although it has experienced a bumpy ride over the years, the Conservative ideology came together long enough to elect Ronald Reagan in 1980.

Chapter 8: The American Conservative Movement 1980-2000, presents the aftermath of the Reagan years: the breakdown of the Conservative ideology, renewed strength of the Left, and the election of Bill Clinton, who used a centrist platform to gain and keep the White House.

Chapter 9: The American Conservative Movement into the 21st Century, describes the presidencies of Bush, Obama, and Trump in relation to the changing American view of the role of government. Conservatives in the 21st Century find themselves on the outside of the culture wars because the Left controls both the media and academia. Conservatives have squandered their opportunities for election success by not being more flexible with regard to social issues.

Chapter 10: Criticizing the Conservative Movement, describes the limits of Conservatism and the blind spots its adherents create for themselves. Conservatives are often criticized for being non-ideological and for stubbornly clinging to the status quo.

Chapter 11: Destroying Tradition, A Case Study, describes in detail the impact of the French Revolution on the development of a modern government in France. The story of France is unique because it is one of the few traditional European societies that completely tore down its social and political fabric in an attempt to reform itself. It remains the most important example of the danger of discarding

Conservative traditions as a framework for moving a society forward.

Chapter 12: Conservatives into the Future, describes the direction of the contemporary Conservative movement as it moves forward. These are difficult times for America and it will take some heavy lifting by Conservatives to help move the country forward in the face of tribalism, global change, and the current pandemic. Conservatives have the important role of applying the brakes on the rapid, seemingly directionless change that will, as history has shown, cause harm to American Society.

CHAPTER TWO

HUMAN EVOLUTION AND INNATE MORALITY

*Who would have imagined that the human brain is
hardwired to be conservative or liberal?*

Anonymous

Human evolutionary origins have been clearly established,
despite remaining controversial, and we understand that the
first organisms on earth emerged billions of years ago.
Hominids appeared along the evolutionary trail as an
advanced species, successors to the primate ancestors they
shared with the chimpanzee. Separating from their common
ancestors some 5 million years ago, the early hominids found
their way out of the jungle to the savannah, leaving their
chimp cousins behind. By 3.6 million years ago, as a result
of their evolved skeletal and cerebral structures, hominids
walked upright. They could also speak and manipulate
objects. As the hominid brain grew in functionality, higher
intelligence, notably verbal and non-verbal communication,
further separated them from the rest of the animal kingdom.
Two hundred thousand years ago, Homo Sapiens emerged
as the final hominid type we see today.

Early human groups were small, numbering 50-100
individuals, featuring the most intelligent or most

charismatic members of the group acting as leaders. There was a rudimentary social class system in which strength, intelligence, and appeal dominated weakness, simplemindedness, and social or physical ineptitude. The weakest and most socially incompatible were ostracized. Human bands maintained an egalitarian structure, driven by an innate human resistance to oppression.

Human beings are social by nature and are more comfortable in a group than when they are alone. Group relationships offer protection for the family unit and additional hands to help perform necessary tasks. At some point in human history, a shared morality developed, based on an accepted set of rules that allowed the group to function and operate smoothly. Social morality was a giant step beyond personal morality because it required humans to suppress selfishness and family priorities to realize the benefits of a relationship with outsiders.

Group morality represented an amalgam of individual moralities and a consensus of acceptable behaviors. It has evolved over time in response to changes in individual and collective behaviors. An example of this in the contemporary world is homosexuality. For most of the last century, homosexuality was illegal, and was considered morally deviant and socially unacceptable. Over time, people became more tolerant and openly accepting of this sexual preference and practice. Laws prohibiting homosexuality were changed because a majority of people wanted them changed.

Human morality combines with evolving traits and communication skills in the creation of new mechanisms for socialization. Theory of mind (TOM), the human sense of the existence of others like oneself, developed as a shortcut to direct communication. Speech followed as a more precise tool for interaction, giving man the capacity to influence others with words. Specialized behaviors, such as gossip, became important tools to validate truth, and help build trust between men.

Man lived a nomadic life for 190 millennia because he had to search for food to eat. That behavior pattern changed when he began to develop agricultural skills and domesticate animals. During the Neolithic Period starting in 10,000 BC, pockets of agricultural activity developed in different places around the world. Mesoamerica, Peru, China, the Indus Valley, Egypt, and Mesopotamia appeared at approximately the same time, demonstrating that man's developing brain was prepared for a more complex lifestyle that could view land, resources, and climate in a different way. Those early farmers prospered when they had access to an alluvial plain -- a large flat space containing sedimentary deposits from rivers. The richness of the soil and moisture made growing crops easier. In Mesopotamia, and other evolving ancient societies, farmers constructed irrigation systems to control the rivers and further improve crop production. Agriculture facilitated a larger population density, so these first large-scale human societies were able to form villages, towns, and cities.

Densely populated spaces required a more complex human

social morality. The old tribal model was discarded because it didn't work in groups with large numbers of strangers. Egalitarianism disappeared and was replaced by social and economic stratification, leading to a rigid hierarchy. Land became the most coveted asset because it could generate income. Land ownership produced wealth, separating those with property from everyone else. Governments came into existence out of necessity because an organization was needed to manage the larger and more complex society. Man created the first governments to exert civil control; later, governments began to manage the economy in order to guarantee the efficient operation of commerce.

The first governments were theocracies because priests, as advisors on religious matters, were respected by their people. Temples that doubled as grain storage facilities were constructed to exert control over the economy. Eventually, as wars became common, theocracies fell away and military leaders became the foundation of secular power. Later, successful leaders made themselves kings by asserting a divine right to rule the people. As the centuries passed, human civilization continued to develop and more advanced models of government emerged. These political systems featured citizens' rights, a radical change from what had come before.

The fall of Rome led to the Dark Ages in Europe, which set back the development of Western Civilization a thousand years. As Europe began to recover, humanist ideas redirected man's thinking toward the individual as the center of society, rather than cultural groups or religions. During the

Enlightenment, man's curiosity about the world led to the expansion of science and the widespread use of technology. Democracy, Capitalism, and freedom of religion followed. Along with these benefits, industrialization brought disruption and exploitation of the worker, accelerating the need for government programs to alleviate rampant inequality.

Today, in the early 21st Century, humans find themselves in a world of disruption where change occurs at a faster rate than they can tolerate; this disruption creates anxiety and dissatisfaction. In America, society's views about morality have split, creating factionalism and tribalism.

Those who are most uncomfortable with rapid change resist it most strongly, arguing for the status quo and honoring traditions as a brake against uncontrolled change. Others, with equal strength, embrace change and view it as necessary. They see the advancement of human society as morally desirable. These conflicting views are not just opinions; they are principles that have developed over time throughout human history, influenced by genetic components.

The Brain and Human Behavior

Although the research is not yet definitive, it is now apparent there is a link between genetics, adaptive biology, and political orientation. In other words, there are genetic factors that influence political behavior through individual personality differences. Research in several disciplines has provided clues as to how this linkage operates.

23

Structural Differences in the Human Brain

A 2011 study by cognitive neuroscientist Ryota Kanai at University College of London,[3] found a correlation between differences in political views and brain structures. Kanai performed MRI scans on the brains of 90 students, each of whom had previously indicated their political orientation on a five-point scale ranging from "very liberal" to "very conservative." Students with more conservative political views tended to have larger amygdalae, those structures deep within the temporal lobes that have a primary role in the processing of emotions, motivations, anxiety, and fear. Kanai found clusters of gray matter significantly associated with conservativism in the left insula and the right entorhinal cortex. The insula is associated with perception, self-awareness, and cognitive functioning. The entorhinal cortex is important for human memory, memory processing, and navigation. Kanai found conservatives were more sensitive to disgust, and this is consistent with increased functionality of the insula.

Liberal students, on the other hand, tended to have larger volumes of grey matter in the anterior cingulate cortex, the structure of the brain associated with monitoring uncertainty and handling conflicting information. This suggests individuals with this characteristic have a higher tolerance for uncertainty and conflicts, and can accept change more easily than others.

---

[3] R. Kanai, "Political Orientations are Correlated," 677.

24

Those findings created an interesting link with the moral foundations of Conservatism and Progressivism, as we will discuss later. In an interview with Live Science, Kanai stressed it was unclear whether these specialized structures in the brain led to the formulation of political views, or whether one's political views contributed to further development of these areas of the brain.

Functional Differences Between People
John Jost (1968-) and others have done significant research in the psychology of political views and have demonstrated that Conservatives and Liberals have different attitudes toward the status quo versus change, and order versus chaos.

Jost, Nosek, and Gosling,[4] showed that political orientation not only predicted attitudes about the importance of tradition and hierarchy versus social change and equality, but also that political orientation predicted automatic associations to a considerable degree. Their study analyzed test subject preferences for values like tradition versus progress; conformity versus rebelliousness; order versus chaos; stability versus flexibility, and traditional values versus change. The researchers demonstrated that most participants preferred order over chaos, but the strength of those preferences was higher among Conservatives. Liberals preferred flexibility over stability and progress over tradition. A large difference between Liberals and Conservatives was also apparent when resistance to change

---

[4] J. T. Jost, et al. "Ideology: Its resurgence in social," 126.

and acceptance of inequality were connected. Conservatives favored traditional values, while Liberals favored change.

Jost also investigated the relationship between political orientation and implicit intergroup attitudes, using established categories for comparison. His results showed that Liberals held stronger egalitarian attitudes than Conservatives. In every case, Liberals were significantly less likely than Conservatives to exhibit preferences for advantaged over disadvantaged groups, such as straights over gays, whites over blacks, or light-skinned over dark-skinned individuals. These findings suggest that Left-Right socio-political differences stem from basic psychological preferences, or that adopting a specific ideology led people to internalize a host of extremely general attitudes concerning stability versus change and hierarchy versus equality.

Another area of study was the heritability of social and political attitudes. Based on data comparing samples of identical and fraternal twins who had been reared apart in the United States and Australia, Alford, Funk, and Hibbing[5] concluded that as much as 40-50% of the statistical variability in ideological opinions could be attributed to genetic factors. The most likely explanation for this is that there are basic psychological predispositions that are partially heritable and can contribute to individual preferences for liberal or conservative ideas.

---

[5] Alford, et al. "Are political orientations," 153.

Jost et al.[6] suggested that ideological differences emerge, at least in part, for psychological reasons. The thesis for this premise is the existence of what the researchers labelled "elective affinities." Not only are there innate psychological differences between people, but there also are a set of social attitudes based on those psychological tendencies. Conservative ideology differs from Liberal ideology in two ways: First, in the Conservative preference for stability and order over social change, and second, in Conservative acceptance of inequality as natural and/or legitimate. The researchers tested whether Conservative preferences for stability and hierarchy would increase whenever uncertainty and threat triggers were increased for innate (dispositional) or temporary (situational) reasons. Stability and hierarchy generate comfort and structure, whereas social change and equality generate discomfort. People appear to avoid the unpredictability associated with social change and increased equality when they are feeling threatened or uncertain. It followed from this that Conservative leaders would be more attractive when a person's need to reduce uncertainty and threat were high. Liberal leaders and opinions would be attractive when the need to reduce uncertainty is low. The data revealed that intolerance of ambiguity and stronger personal needs for order, structure and closure were all positively associated with Conservatism. Openness to new experiences, and tolerance for uncertainty were all positively correlated with Liberalism. The data also revealed that fear of threat and loss, death anxiety, and exposure to systematic threats were associated with Conservatism.

---

[6] Jost, et al. "Political conservatism as," 339.

Jost et al.[7] evaluated the degree of empirical support for two hypotheses: a) that a relationship existed between political views and the need to reduce uncertainty; and b) that the extreme beliefs of those at the ends of the spectrum had the same intensity. Their analysis indicated that a linear relationship existed between political orientation and closed-mindedness. Specifically, as participants became more conservative, their scores on avoidance of uncertainty, intolerance of ambiguity, dogmatism, and mental rigidity increased.

This pattern indicated that extremists on the Left were more closed-minded than moderates on the Left, and moderates on the Left were more closed-minded than centrists. Extremists on the Right were more closed-minded than extremists on the Left and moderates on the Right were more closed-minded than moderates on the Left. In other words, those on the Right tend to be more close-minded than those on the Left.

It is important to make clear that "elective affinities" are not all personality based. There are also situational triggers of "liberal shift" and "conservative shift." A great many studies have shown that highly threatening circumstances tended to increase one's affinity for politically conservative leaders and opinions.

Results from Thorisdottir and Jost[8] indicated that participants scored higher on closed-mindedness when they

---

[7] Ibid. p. 383
[8] Ibid.

completed the terrorism questionnaire with high threat labels. Being randomly assigned to the high threat condition also led participants to rate themselves as more conservative on the ideological self-placement item. Furthermore, closed-mindedness statistically mediated the effect of threat on conservatism, suggesting that cognitive narrowing in response to threat explains the increased affinity for conservative rhetoric and ideology. This work provides the most direct evidence to date that short-term as well as long-term needs to reduce uncertainty and threat play a significant role in determining ideological outcomes, even temporary ones.

Polymorphism

An evolutionary explanation for political and moral diversity is polymorphism, which describes the way a gene can be expressed in multiple ways. Human blood type and gender represent examples of this phenomenon. These variations result from frequency-dependent selection, which has two types: positive and negative. Positive frequency dependent selection means that a gene's fitness increases as it becomes more common. Negative frequency dependent selection means that a gene's fitness decreases as it becomes more common.

Tim Dean (1977-) has suggested that we live in a moral ecosystem whereby the viability of any existing moral approach would be diminished by the destruction of all alternative approaches, which is to say political balance promotes survival of the human species. In other words, a human society could not survive if it had too many liberals or too many conservatives in it. Polymorphism provides the framework for human political views and helps create the individual's morality and political philosophy.[9]

Points to Remember

1. The human brain has developed over time to adapt to a changing social setting. The brain has developed specific tools like speech, to create a more reliable communication system which can be used in interpersonal relationships.

2. Researchers have shown there are physical differences between the brains of Conservatives and Liberals, and those differences influence behavior.

3. The differences in brain function and moral behavior are due to a combination of heritability and exposure to the environment and social groups.

4. Differences between conservatives and liberals are centered in the value of change. Conservatives do not like change and prefer the status quo. Liberals love change and seek lifestyles where change occurs.

5. Liberals can become more conservative if a significant threat such as 9/11 occurs. Threats make them behave like conservatives, at least temporarily.

---

[9] Dean, "Evolution and Moral."

CHAPTER THREE

THE COMPLEX CONSERVATIVE MORALITY

Anyone who values truth should stop worshipping reason.

Jonathan Haidt

Simply stated, morality is a set of rules that attempt to define right and wrong, good and bad, in human society. From the time of the Greeks to the present day, philosophers, psychologists, and religious leaders, searching for the best way to understand and govern human society have studied morality. For at least as long, moral concepts have been built into rules, tenets, and laws to try to influence human behavior toward that ideal.

Jonathan Haidt's (1963-) research on human morality, starting in 1993, applied morality to human behavior. Haidt, who is a moral psychologist, was wondering why people in different cultures appeared to have different moralities. Through his research, Haidt was able to identify five moral foundations that were not only innate in human beings, but also influence their behavior. The array and intensity of those foundations also influences political orientation. Haidt's analysis of data, collected across many cultures, suggested that morality was relative. This variation in people's moral point of view means that individuals at the extremes on the Left and Right have significantly different perceptions of the world.

The five moral foundations are: Caring, Fairness, Loyalty, Authority, and Sanctity.

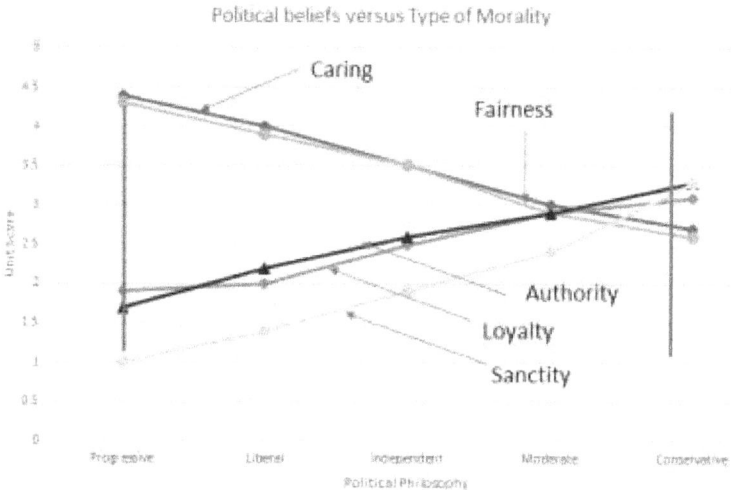

Political beliefs versus Type of Morality

When Haidt asked test subjects to fill out a questionnaire designed to identify the strength of each of their five moral foundations, their answers were expressed as a score between one and five. Constructing a graph using the moral foundation scores demonstrates variations for each foundation based on the subject's political views. Observing the chart above, one can see that the Caring score is higher among Progressives and slopes downward to a lower level for Conservatives. The Authority score is lower for Progressives and rises as it moves to the right to its highest level for Conservatives. One can see Loyalty, Authority, and Sanctity are more important to Conservatives than Liberals. For the Left, morality is about Caring and Fairness, and the other foundations are less important to them. The world is quite different to those on the Right, because Conservatives possess a more complex morality. In this context, "complex" means confusing or complicated. Conservative moral values have close to equal strength, so decision-making requires Conservatives to reconcile competing values. Haidt also identified a sixth moral foundation called Liberty, which acts as supplemental moral foundation working in concert with the others. (Liberty is not included in the chart.)

Moral Foundations of Conservatives
The Loyalty Foundation
Loyalty is defined as acceptance of and respect for an individual, group, or institution. Because man is a social animal, he likes to form groups and participate in group activities. Conservatives show great loyalty in their allegiance to sports teams, memberships in clubs, and affiliated religious activities. They derive psychological benefits from being loyal: a sense of belonging; a sense of being part of something important, and even a reason for being alive. Loyalty is also important for group success. Soldiers must feel and display loyalty to their commanders and obey orders, because disloyalty is likely to put them in harm's way.

The Left discards loyalty as unimportant. To them, loyalty is a trap, leading them to domination by some perceived sinister force. Those on the Left tend to be globalist, while those on the Right are more nationalistic. Patriotic feelings allow the Right to connect Loyalty, Authority, and Liberty to their nation. Those on the Left eschew such sentimental trappings and outward expressions. NFL players kneeling during the National Anthem, beginning in the 2018-19 season, was an ideological unemotional progressive demonstration against the intolerance represented by a symbol of American patriotism.

The Authority Foundation

Authority is acceptance of and respect for a control-based authority, as opposed to a power-based authority or hierarchy. Like Loyalty, Authority evolved because it benefited primitive man. Human groups operate more efficiently in a hierarchy than they do an egalitarian environment. In a hierarchy, the diverse skills of group members are combined to create maximum output. Natural leaders need to lead instead of being followers. Darwin was confused about how the egalitarian model in primitive human society was able to function. He considered it inefficient for man to ignore the value of leaders when they could be used to help the social group operate more efficiently.

Authority also has a dangerous side, which appears when a society grants authority to individuals who harbor immoral intent. Hitler comes to mind as the best example of that phenomenon. Authority is not important to the Left. They distrust this foundation because it is hierarchical, promotes inequality, and is power seeking.

The Sanctity Foundation

Sanctity was originally a warning system to protect human beings from disease, by its association with disgust.

Offensive smells (particularly food), soiled objects, and diseased people have historically triggered a revulsion that demanded avoidance. There is also another side to Sanctity, however, which is the positive expression of veneration for objects that are valued. In that sense, Sanctity represented both unapproachable, untouchable good and unapproachable, untouchable bad. Organized religion has always focused on the sanctity of human life as ordained by God. Objects associated with religion are sanctified: the crucifix, and the star of David are common examples. One does not have to be religious to express sanctity. Fitness advocates sanctify their bodies by avoiding foods or habits that can harm them.

The Liberty Foundation
Liberty is the last of the Conservative foundations, and its enemy is oppression. When human beings feel oppressed, even by those they admire, the need for liberty forms a reaction against that oppression. We recall the words from our colonial days, "Give me liberty or give me death." Today we have protests to "liberate" taxpayers from oppressive taxation. The Libertarian Party seeks to return government to the period of Classic Liberalism, which means small government.

The Liberty foundation is used differently by Liberals and Conservatives. Those on the Left use liberty to seek freedom from oppression and avoid harm (the Caring foundation). They object to the status of victimized groups because those groups are oppressed and have lost their liberty (freedom). Because the Left sees Caring as more important than

Fairness, Fairness has a lower priority. It's the Liberty/Caring combination that rules. For example, if someone commits a crime and goes to jail, those on the Left are sensitive to the punishment given because it causes harm, so harm overrides the fairness of the punishment based on the crime. Leftists will advocate for lighter punishment because they believe people are basically good and their troubles are caused by factors beyond their control. A recent example of this view was the commutation of the death sentence for convicted Boston Marathon bomber Dzhokar Tsarnaev by a Left-leaning judge. Later, the death penalty for the terrorist was reinstated by the ruling of the more conservative Justice Department.

Conservatives feel oppression when their liberty has been unjustly taken away by government. This can take the form of laws that restrict them from doing things they wish to do, or the taking of their money to fund government programs that offer no benefit to them. Unfairness comes into play when one specific group receives government benefits and other groups, are excluded from those benefits.

The four foundations outlined here complicate decision making for Conservatives when they come into conflict with each other. Loyalty can stand alone or be paired with Authority if the group is hierarchical. Authority is often based on tradition, which is the respect for institutions that are long-standing and provide stability. Sanctity is the veneration of ideas or objects most often in a group setting, such as religion. Within a group, the sense of liberty promotes a balance between freedom and authority. Loyalty and authority can be compromised by a loss of liberty, but liberty can be ignored if loyalty and authority are strong enough. Throughout history, kings sought to validate their authority, through tradition and sanctions provided the church. Nearly a century ago, the German people traded liberty for authority when they chose the Nazis as the majority party in the German government over the Communists and Social Democrats.

Examples of Conservative Moral Conflicts
Politics – Authority Versus Loyalty

Government is a legal authority exerting power granted by the citizens of a nation. Loyalty to an authority is dependent on its behavior. When Conservatives see government behaving in an unacceptable manner, their loyalty to it comes into question. Depending on their level of anger, they may criticize the government or change who they vote for in the next election. Conservatives like to pair authority and loyalty because they prefer order and order comes from strong authority.

Same Sex Marriage – Sanctity versus Loyalty

In 2015, the United States Supreme Court legalized same-sex marriage across the United States. The decision in Obergefell v. Hodges[10] affirmed that same-sex marriage is a fundamental right under the U.S. Constitution. Some Conservatives disagree with this law because, to them, it violates the sanctity of their religious principles, which define marriage in the traditional sense, between a man and a woman. If their elected representative supports the new

---

[10] Obergefell v. Hodges, 576 U.S. 644 (2015)

law, the constituents may be drawn into a conflict between two moral foundations: Sanctity and Loyalty. If the concept of sanctity of marriage is more important to them than loyalty to their Congressman, they may decide to support a different candidate in the future.

Raising Taxes – Liberty versus Loyalty

Congresspersons enjoy great loyalty among their followers. If one of them introduces a bill to raise taxes and it passes, some Conservative constituents will feel their liberty is being compromised by government taking their income. Loss of liberty may be more important to them than the loyalty they feel toward their representative, so they may switch their vote in the next election.

Conservative Sub-groups
Strongly focused on Liberty

Conservative sub-groups consist of individuals who have an unusual imbalance between their moral foundations. Libertarians have an outsized Liberty foundation, so they oppose any government action that compromises liberty, like taxation. They do not like big government and want to limit its size because, in their view, government destroys liberty through wealth transfer and the expansion of unnecessary programs. Libertarians oppose the Left because of its support of the welfare state. Libertarians also despise foreign policy because they see it as wasteful and outside of government responsibility. Perhaps the most extreme case of a Liberty foundation is when individuals live off the grid and survive in the wilderness and seek total control of their lives in a place where no government can interfere.

Strongly Focused on Loyalty

A second sub-group includes strong loyalists who unerringly follow a leader or group. Individuals with a strong nationalistic feeling, are driven to accept a leader's authority without question. Loyalty is a component of patriotism, which is based on believing in one's country and the principles it stands for. The loyalty created by Trump, the populist, generated tremendous enthusiasm for him as someone who cared about the issues important to constituents, particularly those who like loyalty to authority.

Strongly Focused on Authority

A third group of Conservatives are those who strongly embrace Authority. They are most comfortable operating in a social hierarchy where there is strong leadership. They understand and accept their own position in the hierarchy. Some people can be leaders but others cannot. Those who cannot lead are happy to let others lead, and feel less pressure because they don't want the responsibility of leading. They connect to the power generated by the authoritarian structure.

Strongly Focused on Sanctity

A fourth Conservative type includes those with an outsized Sanctity foundation. In the case of religious people, the value of religion and religious symbols becomes paramount in their lives. If the religion and its veneration of symbols are strong enough, followers may choose to dedicate their lives to the church. Those on the Left tend to discount traditional religions, but have secular religions of their own. For example, fanatical environmentalists put their feelings about the sanctity of the earth ahead of other social priorities. Their goal is so important that they overlook the difficulties standing in the way of achieving that goal.

Conservatives' View of their Morality as it Relates to American Politics Today

In 2018, *More in Common*, published a study to analyze the political views of the American people.[11] It collected questionnaires from nearly 8,000 respondents with a goal of identifying core beliefs of individual Americans, including moral values, social values, and political ideology. They applied cluster analysis to the data to identify possible grouping trends, and the analysis showed 7 different factions make up the American electorate: 1) Progressive Activists; 2) Traditional Liberals; 3) Passive Liberals; 4) politically disengaged; 5) Moderates; 6) Traditional Conservatives; and 7) devoted Conservatives.

Conservatives sit on the right of the political spectrum, and to the right of the moderates who are less ideological. Conservatism has two groups: traditional and devoted. Simply put, traditionalists embrace the Conservative ideology but are tolerant about opposing views. They understand that compromise is necessary in politics. Devoted Conservatives are not flexible; they wholly embrace ideological views they feel should not be compromised.

---

[11] Hawkins, et al. "Hidden Tribes." 2018.

Traditional Conservatives (19% of the population – 62 million people) feel America's foundations are under attack from a liberal political culture that emphasizes diversity and downplays American accomplishments. They believe in values like personal responsibility and self-reliance; they think too much attention is given to issues of gay rights, sexual harassment, and racism. They have a clear sense of identity as Americans, as Christians, and as Conservatives, but they are not as strident in their beliefs as devoted Conservatives. For example, traditional Conservatives are open to dialogue or compromise on a pathway to citizenship for undocumented immigrants brought here as children. They acknowledge that racism and racist acts persist in the United States. They are suspicious of the traditional media, yet they are more likely than any other group to feel their voice is represented in American politics. Of traditional Conservatives at the time of the research:

- Less than half (47%) say the country is rigged in favor of the rich and Powerful.
- Forty-six percent feel they have a say in politics.
- Twenty-three percent say having two American parents is a very important part of being American.
- Forty-nine percent strongly approve of Donald Trump's job performance.
- Forty-one percent watch Fox News - and 25% listen to talk radio.
- Seventy-nine percent are white.
- Sixty-five percent are older than 65.
- Their education is similar to that of the average American.

Devoted Conservatives (6% of the population – 20 million) are equivalent to the Progressive activists at the other end of the political spectrum. Like Progressives, devoted Conservatives are happy and secure in life. They see American traditions under assault and feel they are under attack from the media, which is pushing Liberal dogma. They see themselves as defenders of American values they believe are rapidly eroding.

- Sixty-three percent list politics as a hobby.
- Seventy-five percent strongly support a US-Mexico border wall.
- Sixty-four percent have donated to their place of worship.
- Eighty-eight percent strongly supported a "Muslim travel ban."
- Sixty-three percent oppose ideological compromise.
- Eighty-eight percent are white.
- Sixty-five percent are older than 65.
- Eleven percent were born between 1985 and 2000.
- Forty-five percent come from the South.

Both groups value the traditions that have provided the foundation for the Conservative belief system. Their concept of authority links the Constitution to the present. They are willing to grant politicians authority, as long as their efforts are directed toward Conservative goals. They sanctify the traditions of the United States.

The main difference between the two groups is the devoted Conservatives' resistance to *any* change. That makes them bad candidates for involvement in practical solutions to move the country forward. They don't care to debate the correctness of their positions.

Points to Remember

1. Unlike Liberals, Conservatives have a complex morality based on competing moral foundations.

2. Loyalty, Authority, Sanctity, and Liberty are key components of a conservative moral view.

3. Conservatives must reconcile their competing moral foundations when they make decisions.

4. There some Conservative groups that have unbalanced moral foundations, meaning that one foundation dominates the others. For example, a person might put loyalty above authority, sanctity, or liberty and make decisions based on that one foundation.

5. A fundamental motivator for Conservatives is resistance to rapid change. Conservatives honor tradition and view it as a necessary framework for change.

6. Conservatives view equality differently than liberals do. They believe a hierarchical society is the most natural form of human society and true equality is unachievable.

CHAPTER FOUR

CONSERVATISM BEFORE THE ENLIGHTENMENT

The wise men of antiquity, when they wished to make the whole world peaceful and happy, first put their own States into proper order. Before putting their States into proper order, they regulated their own families. Before regulating their families, they regulated themselves. Before regulating themselves, they tried to be sincere in their thoughts. Before being sincere in their thoughts, they tried to see things exactly as they really were.

Confucius

The core of the word "conservatism" is "conserve," which refers to preserving the valuable and valued experiences of human society from the past and present. This means avoiding economic and social conditions an individual sees as disruptive or inappropriate to what is being conserved. Conservatives embrace social continuity over time as a stabilizing factor for human society.

Conservatism in the Primitive World

In a previous chapter, I described Conservatism as the behavior resulting from an enhanced expression of a brain-based warning system developed to protect the life of primitive man. This function is formed in the fight/flight part of the brain called the amygdala, among related structures. All human beings and most animals have the fight/flight function, but among humans it is more developed in Conservatives. That primitive brain mechanism makes them more cautious than their non-Conservative peers and is driven by the Conservative Gene.

To see how this may have worked in the prehistoric era, consider an example: A group of tribesmen plan to go hunting for meat, in this case for a large animal or group of animals that can feed the tribe. The previous day, a scout observed a herd of pigs nearby. He also observed a few lions in the area. The hunters discuss among themselves how to conduct the hunt. Some of the would-be hunters were anxious to begin and looked forward to it, seeing the hunt as an opportunity to bask in the recognition that would come with a successful outcome. Other would-be hunters were more circumspect; they hungered for the pork but were worried about the lions. They remembered a recent hunt in which three of their fellow tribesmen had been killed suddenly by lions. The second group suggested scouts observe the herd of pigs for a day or two longer to see if the lions remained in the area. The anxious hunters didn't like that idea; they felt it was overly cautious and a waste of time. Ultimately, tribal leaders settled the disagreement and approved the hunt to occur immediately.

These opposing positions had the same goal: feed the tribe. Differences in approach were partly due to the presence of the distribution of brain function and the influence it had on attitudes and behaviors related to success. Those with the first, more impetuous point of view, sought the joy of a new experience and disregarded the risks. Immediate action implied success. Those with the second, more cautious point of view, based their opinion on innate risk analysis and wanted to use caution. This spectrum of attitudes toward success represented the natural variation in human attitudes. The tribe did not just consist of extremes, however. There were others in the middle who were more flexible than the cautious conservatives, and more conservative than the liberals.

Human survival depended on a cross-section of risk acceptance for obvious reasons. Any group consisting only of liberals would be wiped out in short order, due to faulty and dangerous risk-taking. Any group consisting only of conservatives would avoid risk in situations that warranted change, so their hesitation would have created missed opportunities.

Conservatism in the Ancient World
The Neolithic period (starting in 10,000 BC) saw rapid changes in man's social structure, because human societies were needed to implement agriculture and the domestication of animals. The primitive roles of change agent/status quo advocate had to adapt to fit new, larger, and denser human social groups. The individual's ability to influence change was severely limited, based on his small sphere of influence. Changes impacting the individual were now determined by a hierarchical government structure that operated outside the individual's personal and familial space.

Acts of government affected people positively, negatively, or not at all. People reacted most strongly when the impact of government was negative. For example, when taxes were raised, taking more money for the government, the people's income was impacted. Beyond the government's impact on them as individuals, each person had their own perception of whether their society was on a positive or negative trajectory. That perception was based on whether society's path matched their own moral belief system. If liberal, they would expect society to adopt changes to make progress toward a world the individual would see as an improvement over the current one. If conservative, the individual would expect the government to adopt a pace of change that minimized the risk of disruption and instability.

In the ancient world, power was concentrated at the top. A king or ruler would exercise his power through alliances with aristocrats and wealthy men. As long as his programs benefited his allies, his position was secure. When he failed in executing that task, he would become vulnerable. Those on the bottom of the socio-economic ladder could object to government action, but lacked the power to do anything about it. This centralized society was Darwinian. Property and money created power, replacing muscles and weapons. Those who possessed the greatest capacity to accumulate wealth were the winners and the powerful. Women and those disadvantaged by nature, such as the mentally deficient, or physically disabled, could not compete.

Historically, power was concentrated in the hands of Conservatives. Those who possessed wealth and power tended toward Conservatism because they believed the status quo posed less risk to their positions. Recall that the moral foundations that drive Conservatives include respect for Authority, group Loyalty, and Sanctity. They were consistent with a respect for power and power relationships, and loyalty to authority figures, such as a monarch. Sanctity was tradition-based, such as a respect for hereditary authority, and were enhanced when religious leaders sanctioned the monarch. Liberty was unknown in the ancient world. Most citizens had no rights and could not exert any control over government. Liberty came later as an Enlightenment concept, when the individual was granted standing for the first time in history.

Conservatism, in the ancient world, was a personal philosophy made up of two components: Biological conservatism and respect for tradition. The biological component drove the desire for the status quo and was based on the conservative mind expressing caution and being averse to risk. Tradition augmented conservative thinking by respecting cultural behaviors that had been repeated over generations and centuries. Traditions offered stability and continuity to society. Traditions also acted as a brake against rapid change which could be socially disrupting.

Greek Conservatism
The Greeks created the science of progress when they began conceptualizing, inventing, and implementing new ideas. Progress, as they saw it, resulted from using creativity to acquire knowledge. Wisdom came from "knowledge" and served as the foundation for a moral life.

49

The Greek attraction to undiscovered knowledge drove them to take an orderly approach to mastering a discipline. In Hellenic thought, there was always a desire for change, as a reaction against national ideals. Diodorus, the great Greek historian of the 1st Century BC, complained that the Greeks spent too much of their time redefining philosophy because they never accepted the results of their predecessors. That lack of a final definition, caused the souls of the philosophers to exist in a state of continuous oscillation.

The Greek study of individualism began with Aristotle (385-323 BCE). Aristotle is often cited for believing morality and politics, unlike natural science, lacked special experts; human experience over generations was the main source of knowledge in those areas.

Greek Conservatism enhanced belief in a glorious past and a natural order. As innovative as the Greeks were, their Conservatism coexisted with change, even extreme change, as seen in their constantly changing democracy. Greek Conservatism was about preserving traditional and natural ways. Using a democratic process to achieve conservative ideals was not only possible, but it also was the most effective path forward. The ability to balance new and old implied Conservatism was more than just a political behavior. Had it been so, conflicting political beliefs could not have coexisted. Conservatism was, and remains, a cultural belief in a specific way of life; as long as there is culture, there will always be people who seek to protect it against the changing world.

Focus on the Hellenic desire for change obscured the conservative tendencies of Greek life, which were strongly tied to tradition. Because the Hellenic ideal had such a great influence on the modern world, we tend to focus on new ideas as the most important contribution of the Greeks and ignore Greek Conservatism.

The Hellenistic Age (323 BC – 30 BC), which followed the time of Alexander the Great, was characterized by the decline of the city-state; the centralization of power; the disintegration of a common faith, and the rise of philosophical asceticism. These factors created an individualism that made man more conscious of himself. He became impatient with the restrictions of society and his literature became more individualistic. Oddly, this philosophical treatment of individualism was foreign to the traditional Greek society because Greek life was largely institutional. As such, it was subject to the dictates of a national point of view. Greek philosophers spoke of national ideals, though there was neither a single Greek nation, nor a common Hellenic typology in art, language, or literature.

The Greeks were devoted to tradition in a surprising way, given their affinity for what was new. They were intolerant of repression, yet they considered dissent regarding philosophical teachings inappropriate.

Roman Conservatism

In both thought and action, the Romans were polar opposites to the Greeks. Practical people focused on their agrarian world; the Romans were not interested in taking the time for philosophical thought. They were builders, not thinkers, and were interested in creating the structures needed to make life easier, not in idly thinking about the existence of man for which the Greeks were known. A useful analogy might be found by comparing the Greeks and Romans to the French and Germans. The French are more philosophical and tend toward idealism. The Germans devote themselves to structure and organization. The French were stimulated by the Enlightenment to tear down their political system as an attempt to start over; Germans rejected the Enlightenment outright as a dangerous attack on their status quo.

In the Roman Republican government, the Senate was the most conservative body. Its members were wealthy and powerful, intent on doing what was necessary to protect their status. Although it contained both liberal and conservative factions, the Senate always acted to conserve itself and the power it held over the Roman people. Eventually, hubris and mismanagement of the Republic cost the Senators their power when military men used the army to take control of the government.

After 135 BC, during a period of great civil unrest over the problem of poverty, political factions began to emerge. During that time, the brothers Tiberius and Gaius Gracchi, were elected as tribunes of the people. Their passion for the disadvantaged drove the brothers to try to pass an agrarian law to provide free land to the poor. The Senate's response was to label them power hungry and to plot against them. Optimates, a Senate supporting faction, also appeared and began to work on the Senate's behalf. The Plebeians put forward their own counter faction called the Populares, or people's men.

After a series of confrontations between the factions, each of the brothers ran for reelection. Both were assassinated by agents of the Senate. For the next 80 years, Roman politics was marked by the confrontation between these factions. The Optimates favored the ancestral Roman laws and customs, as well as the supremacy of the Senate over the popular assemblies and the tribunes. The Populares fought for expanding the rights of the people, to give them equal standing with the ruling class.

The Optimates' cause reached its peak under the dictatorship of Lucius Cornelius Sulla in 81 BC. Sulla stripped the people's assemblies of their power, raised the number of members of the Senate from 300 to 600, and executed many Populares whose names were taken from lists of enemies. After Sulla's withdrawal from public life in 80 BC, his policies were reversed. Later, Pompey found himself as the leader of the Optimates' faction when the civil war with Julius Caesar began in 49 BC. Caesar was considered the man of the people so Pompey was forced to act against his own interests. When Caesar came to power, he worked to eliminate the factions because they represented a threat to his rule. He was ultimately unsuccessful and the Optimates, along with disillusioned Populares, in an attempt to save the Republic, carried out Caesar's assassination in 44 BC. Over the next few years, political factions were swept away by rise of the empire.

When Augustus came to power in 30 BC, he created a unique political system, an authoritarian dictatorship disguised as a Republic. Augustus pretended to revive conservative traditions to legitimize his hold on power.

Conservatism in the Medieval World
Roman Catholic Conservatism
In Western culture, the Roman Catholic Church has stood as a bastion of tradition, having fought to conserve the tenets of its faith for two thousand years. Initially, the Catholic Church survived by winning the war between itself and a group of opposing Christian factions who appeared after the death of Jesus. The Catholics prevailed by ruthlessly enforcing their dogma and attacking all who opposed it.

Once the Dark Ages had passed, the monarchies of England, France, and Germany aligned with the Pope and served as guardians of the European religious tradition. That alliance lasted until the early 16th Century when Martin Luther posted his 95 theses (Disputation of the Power and Efficacy of Indulgences), launching the Protestant Reformation, splitting the church, and facilitating the expansion of new religions in Europe. The Catholic Church's final attempt to retain power was its active participation in the Thirty Years War (1618-1648). Its allies were defeated and the church's power diminished further with the signing of the Treaty of Westphalia. That treaty put Lutheranism and Calvinism on equal status with Catholicism.

Historically, the Catholic Church had operated with two personalities: Conservative in its desire to protect the status quo, its traditions, and its power, and more progressive in its efforts to protect the poor and disadvantaged. Today's Catholic Church has a conservative faction which opposes modernization. This is another example of a battle between the status quo and change. How much change is acceptable? How fast can change occur without permanent damage to an institution built on tradition?

Tradition
Traditions are beliefs or behaviors with symbolic meanings that are passed down within a group or society and express a connection with the past. Common examples include holidays or impractical but socio-historically meaningful clothes, like lawyers' wigs or military officers' spurs. The word "tradition" comes from the Latin *tradere* which means to transmit, to hand over, or to give for safekeeping.

The concept of tradition, as the notion of assigning value to a previous time, is also found in political and philosophical discourse. Political traditions, including constitutions and laws, form the basis on which humans are governed, laws are applied, and institutions thrive or die. Opposing them are counter forces which attack traditions. These forces include industrialization, globalization, and automation.

Originally, traditions were passed orally, pictorially and musically before formal writing systems existed. Tools invented to aid this process include poetic devices, such as rhyme and alliteration.

Tradition changes slowly from one generation to the next, so individuals living out their traditions may not notice changes that occur during their lifetime. For example, when the first interstate highways were built, it took a while for people to realize that having good roads meant they could take vacations farther from home.

Traditions are varied and can include the forms of artistic heritage of a culture; beliefs or customs instituted and maintained by societies and governments, such as national anthems and federal holidays in the United States, and traditions maintained by religious denominations and church bodies that share history, customs, and culture. For example, one can speak of Islam's tradition or Christianity's tradition. Many objects, beliefs and customs can be traditional. Rituals of social interaction can be traditional, with phrases and gestures such as saying "thank you," or sending birth announcements and greeting cards. Tradition can also refer to larger concepts practiced by groups, like family traditions at Christmas, company picnics, and service groups and societies. Some of the oldest traditions include monotheism (3000 years) and citizenship (2000 years).

The term "invention of tradition," was introduced by E. J. Hobsbawm (1917-2012) and refers to presenting a new practice or object in a manner that implies a connection with the past which no longer exists. A tradition may be deliberately created and popularized for personal, commercial, political, or national self-interest, as was done in colonial Africa in the 19th Century. There, craft unionism was invented as a tradition for white mine workers in order to exclude blacks, because they did not share the same history. Traditions may be adopted rapidly, based on a single, highly-publicized event, rather than developing and spreading organically in a population. An example is the wearing of a white wedding dress for first time brides. Queen Victoria wore a white gown at her wedding in 1840, the idea became popular, and it carries on to the present day. Another example of an invention of tradition is the rebuilding of the Palace of Westminster, where the British Parliament is located. The reconstruction created a structure in the original Gothic style, even though the traditions associated with British Democracy only dated to the 19th Century.

The concepts of tradition and traditional beliefs are frequently used in political and religious discourse to establish the legitimacy of particular values. In the United States, the Constitution stands as a great example of a tradition that has been sanctified. Its authors are lauded as great men who helped make the success of our country possible. The document itself is seen as foundational and perpetually valuable as a guide to preserving and carrying the country forward.

Tradition has long been a factor in politics because right-wing parties retain a stronger affinity for the past than left-wing parties. The past is part of the political philosophy of traditionalists, who are focused on the need for the principles of natural law, moral order, hierarchy, organic unity, and intersecting spheres of loyalty. Traditionalists reject the notions of individualism, Liberalism, modernity, and social progress, favoring the church, family, state, and local community. This is the view that is often criticized by the Left because, in their view, traditions are an impediment to progress.

In some societies, especially ones experiencing rapid social change, the idea of "traditional" may be widely contested, with different groups striving to establish their own values as the legitimate ones. Defining and enacting traditions in some cases can be a means of building unity between subgroups in a diverse society; it can also mean tradition is a way of ordering and keeping groups distinctly apart from one another. The Conservative Gene identified traditions as a valuable addition to the conservative thought process because it reinforced stability as a desirable component of human society.

Tradition and the Social Sciences
In the social sciences, tradition is often contrasted with modernity. This dichotomy is generally associated with a model of social change in which societies progress from traditional to modern. Tradition-oriented societies have been characterized as valuing piety, harmony, group welfare, stability, and interdependence, while societies exhibiting modernity tend to value individualism, mobility, and progress. Anthony Giddens (1938-) saw tradition as something bound to ritual; in turn, ritual guarantees its continuation. Others have criticized this dichotomy as oversimplified, arguing tradition is dynamic, heterogeneous, and coexists successfully with modernity even within individuals

Tradition has to be separated from customs, conventions, laws, norms, routines, and rules. Tradition is allegedly invariable, while the other representations are thought to be more flexible and subject to innovation and change. While the justification for tradition is ideological, the justification for other customs is more practical or technical. Over time, customs, conventions, laws, norms, routines and rules may evolve into traditions, but that generally occurs after they no longer have a practical purpose.

Purposeful Preservation
In many countries, there are concerted attempts to preserve traditions that are at risk of being lost. It has been used to defend the preservation and reintroduction of minority languages such as Cornish under the auspices of the European Charter for Regional or Minority Languages. This organization, founded in 1992, documents and protects the traditions embodied in languages to ensure the public is able to hear speakers in their own languages.

Traditionalism-Conservative Link
Because Conservatives advocate for the status quo, tradition has become a fundamental building block of their ideology. Conservatives recognize the world must change, but they see traditions as the stable time-tested roadmap for change. Conservatives worry when traditions are abandoned on a wholesale basis, as they were during the French Revolution, so that the resulting instability will destroy a society.

Points to Remember

1. Conservatism before the Enlightenment was limited to a natural resistance to change along with the guarding of traditions.

2. Conservatives affinity for Loyalty, Authority, and Sanctity became a driving force for government control as the first societies emerged. Monarchs acted conservativity to protect their power and validate their hereditary line.

3. In the time of the Greeks and Romans, elements of Liberalism first appeared, working for changes in society that would benefit the common people.

4. During the Enlightenment Period, a new role for the individual in society was created, and that role opposed many established traditions. Conservatives fought against that change.

5. Traditions are an aspect of human society which help to conserve elements of a culture. They act as a brake against too much change, and serve as guideposts for the path forward.

CHAPTER FIVE

CONSERVATISM BECOMES POLITICAL

It is a general popular error to suppose the loudest complainers for the public to be the most anxious for its welfare

Edmund Burke

As a political idea, Conservatism had its origin in the United Kingdom near the end of the Enlightenment period. Before that time, it was nothing more than the expression of a biological behavior and socio-cultural belief embracing the status quo and traditions. Conservatism had no political or ideological connection.

The Prologue to Political Conservatism

The 17th Century was a time of enormous upheaval in Great Britain as the growing power of Parliament clashed with the traditional power of the royals. In 1625, Charles I ascended to the throne at age 25. He immediately began to quarrel with a Parliament that sought to curb his power, and question his assertion of the historically traditional "divine right" of rule. The British people objected to the King's claim he could raise taxes without the consent of Parliament and grew to resent him as a power-hungry tyrant. His marriage to a

Catholic made him unacceptable to the Puritans and other protestant groups.

In 1642, civil war broke out and lasted for three years until Charles surrendered his army and was handed over to the English Parliament. In spite of his defeat, Charles refused to accept Parliament's creation of a constitutional monarchy and plotted against the government. In 1647, he formed an alliance with Scottish forces and attacked England. His forces were defeated by the army of Oliver Cromwell in 1648, and he was executed for high treason in January 1649.

Cromwell declared England to be a republic and Parliament named the new government a Commonwealth on May 19, 1649. Its Parliament, acquired the nickname "Rump," when loyalist members were purged in December 1648, leaving only part of the original body intact. The remaining members had indicated their loyalty to the republic. Parliament abolished the House of Lords and Privy Council, establishing an English Council of State as the new executive branch. The new Parliament derived power from an association with the army, but that would turn out to be an unstable relationship that recalled the power struggles of the Roman Republic.

The Rump Parliament contained many factions that were constantly at odds with one another. The traditional ruling class regarded it as an illegal government of amateurs, but they also understood the Rump was all that stood between England and the dictatorship of Cromwell. Wisely, the new government aligned itself with the British Constitution, which provided the stability needed to carry England through the greatest period of internal strife in its history.

In July 1653, Cromwell dismissed the Rump Parliament for unknown reasons. Perhaps he was concerned it would attempt to create an alternative government designed to reduce his power. He created a new "Barebones" Parliament, consisting of members nominated by officers of the army. Deposed members of Parliament ridiculed the newcomers as a body of inferior men, but there were, in fact, many who were well-qualified.

As a prelude to future party divisions, the new Parliament split into three factions: 25% were radicals advocating a new political system; 45% wanted modifications to the old system, and the remaining 30% were conservatives who wanted to continue the status quo. Cromwell naïvely believed this disorganized group could come together and create a new constitution. Instead, they fought among themselves and were not able to make any progress. In December 1653, Cromwell dissolved Parliament and put in place a protectorate, naming himself Lord Protector. His authority was granted under a new constitution called the "Instrument of Government."

In 1658, Cromwell died and his son Richard replaced him. Richard did not have the confidence of the army and resigned from office on May 19, 1659. The army then reinstated the Rump Parliament in place of the government of the Commonwealth. Sensing an opportunity, the restored Parliament stripped the power of the army by naming a military council under control of the Speaker of Parliament. While that was going on, Charles II, brother of the executed former king and an exile in the Netherlands, responded to a message from the commander of monarchist forces in Scotland saying he would accept the crown, under certain conditions. On May 8, 1660 Parliament declared that Charles II had been the lawful monarch of England since the execution of Charles I in 1649. Charles II entered London on his birthday, May 29, 1660, and assumed the throne as King of England.

Conservative Ideas Emerge

After Charles came to power, the first threads of a Conservative political philosophy emerged as a result of the Tory movement. Tories supported a hierarchical society featuring a monarch who ruled by divine right. They opposed the idea that sovereignty could be derived from the people, rejecting the authority of Parliament and its support of freedom of religion. Conservatism, as the Tories saw it, was the expression of a desire to retain the old monarchy.

Charles II died in 1685. When his Catholic son James took the throne, the old religious wars flared up again. Anti-Catholics supported an invasion by William III of Orange in 1688 and the monarchy of James came to an end. William became co-regent with his wife Mary, who was the actual heir to the throne. This transition was called the Glorious Revolution because it led to the creation of a new English Bill of Rights and a Constitution that would end the power of the monarchs forever. The change in government toppled the Tories, stripped away the legitimacy of their political views, and left the Whig Party in control of government. To survive, the Tories reformed their movement, agreeing that sovereignty should be vested in the three estates of Crown, Lords, and Commons rather than solely in the Crown. Despite their pivot, the Tories were marginalized during the long period of Whig ascendancy into the 18th Century.

The First Conservatives

English Conservatives often name Richard Hooker (1554–1600) as the founding father of Conservatism, along with David Hume (1711–1776) and Edmund Burke. Hooker, a priest of the Church of England, argued that human beings are naturally inclined to live in society, so governments must be based on this social instinct. In other words, government must respect the elements of the human social system, including the family, and its traditions.

Hume, in addition to his important work in philosophy, had strong beliefs about government. His political views had both conservative and liberal elements, which left them open to interpretation. For example, Hume's history book was banned from the University of Virginia by Thomas Jefferson who labelled it as "too Tory." Hume was suspicious of attempts to reform societies using anything but long-established methods; he asserted that tradition and custom were the best tools for that purpose. Hume has been labelled a "precautionary" Conservative because he advocated change only when the consequences of that change were well understood.

Edmund Burke's legacy labels him as the father of Anti-Enlightenment criticism, even though his views contained both liberal and conservative elements. In a narrow sense, Burkean Conservatism can be characterized as a philosophy which mistrusts a priori reasoning and revolution, preferring the application of experience to tried and tested social structures. Burke rejected political philosophies that advocated the invention of new rights, as manifested most dramatically in the French Jacobin dream of destroying and rebuilding society. Burke held there was practical wisdom in institutions that was passed down through their traditions.

Burke was a leading theorist in his day, finding extreme idealism (Tory or Whig) an endangerment to broader liberties. Like Hume, he rejected abstract reason as an unsound guide for political theory. Burke supported the liberal ideals of private property and the economics of Adam Smith (1723–1790), but thought economics should remain subordinate to a conservative social ethic. Burke further believed capitalism should be subordinate to social traditions and the business class should be subordinate to the aristocracy. He insisted on standards of honor derived from the aristocratic tradition, and saw the aristocracy as the nation's natural leaders. The powers of the Crown should be limited because members of Parliament were more capable than individuals chosen by the monarch.

Revolutionary Jacobinism was Conservatism's polar opposite and historic adversary. The name came from the Jacobin Club, whose central figure, Robespierre (1758-94), launched the French Revolution's Reign of Terror.

Conservatives like Burke made a point of contrasting the French Revolution with England's more peaceful Glorious Revolution of 1688. France experienced a revolution in the original sense; it was a return to a society that existed before its monarchy. In England, traditional institutions were overturned in accordance with a rational plan. Conservatism and revolutionary Jacobinism were inter-dependent concepts that arose together, in conjunction with Liberalism and Socialism. The Enlightenment questioned the natural order and social hierarchy that were previously in place. Implicit in Jacobinism was revolutionary Utopianism, which allowed the sacrifice of present generations for alleged future benefit.

The ideas of men like Hooker and Burke demonstrated the next stage in human application of the Conservative Gene. Conservatives were driven to find ways to connect their beliefs to the new political landscape that would see politicians representing groups. Conservatives needed politicians in office who would represent their views and protect them against forces that would attack them.

Conservative Awakening

Conservatism in England evolved after 1820, embracing free trade in 1846, and a commitment to democracy. This philosophical change strengthened it as a grassroots political force. Conservatism was no longer the philosophical defense of the landed aristocracy, but was now committed to the ideals of both secular and religious order, expanding imperialism, a strengthened monarchy, and a more generous vision of the welfare state, as opposed to the punitive vision of the Whigs and Liberals. As early as 1835, Prime Minister

Benjamin Disraeli (1804-81) attacked the Whigs as overly devoted to an industrial oligarchy, while he described his fellow Tories as the only real democratic party in England. Disraeli played a central role in the creation of the modern Conservative Party, defining its policies and broad outreach. He made the Conservatives the party most identified with the glory and power of the British Empire.

Despite great leadership, there was tension in the Conservative Party between the growing numbers of wealthy businessmen on the one side, and the aristocracy and rural gentry on the other. This tension began to abate when businessmen discovered they could use their wealth to buy titles and country estates, and join the ruling class. Some Conservatives lamented the passing of a pastoral world in which the image of an amoral elite class had earned respect from the lower classes. They viewed the Anglican Church and the aristocracy as balances against commercial wealth, so they worked toward legislation to improve working conditions and urban housing.

In 1834, Tory Prime Minister Robert Peel (1788-1850) issued the Tamworth Manifesto which was a pledge to endorse moderate political reform. This marked the beginning of the transformation of British Conservatism from High Tory Reactionism (supporting low taxes, less military, and the monarchy) towards a more modern form based on "conservation." As a result, the party became known as the Conservative Party, a name it has retained to this day. Peel, however, would also be the root of a split in the party between the traditional Tories, led by the Earl of

Derby and Benjamin Disraeli, and the "Peelites," led first by Peel himself, then by the Earl of Aberdeen. The split occurred in 1846 over the issue of free trade, which Peel supported, versus protectionism, supported by Derby. The majority of party members sided with Derby, while about a third split away, merging with the Whigs and the radicals to form the Liberal Party. Eventually, the Conservative Party would overcome its resistance to protectionism by accepting the Doctrine of Free Trade in 1852.

In the second half of the 19th Century, the Liberal Party faced political schisms, especially over Irish Home Rule. Leader William Gladstone (1809-1898), himself a former Peelite, sought to give Ireland a degree of autonomy, a move opposed by elements in both the Left and Right wings of his party. These factions split off to become the Liberal Unionists, led by Joseph Chamberlain (1836-1914), and formed a coalition with the Conservatives before merging with them in 1912. By the late 19th Century, the traditional business supporters of the UK Liberal Party had joined the Conservatives, making them the party of business and commerce.

Conservatism in Germany

German Conservatism emerged in the first half of the 19th Century after the fall of Napoleon, and was highlighted by two periods: The Age of Metternich and The Age of Bismarck. The Age of Metternich (1815-1848) marked the period from the fall of Napoleon to the March Revolution of 1848. The Age of Bismarck ran from 1862 to 1890.

Germans hated the perspectives, tenets, and foundations of the Enlightenment from its onset in 1650. They saw it tearing down German traditions and attacking the Catholic religion. The French Revolution and the rise of Napoleon, they believed, were direct result of the Enlightenment. Consequently, Germany was forced to endure Napoleon's invasion and occupation of their land.

After Napoleon was defeated in 1815, European leaders, principally Lord Castlereagh the British Foreign Secretary and Prince Metternich, the Austrian Chancellor, implemented the Conservative Order, a policy of cooperation between France's principal enemies. Its purpose was to control the Liberal tide that was sweeping Europe. The participants divided power, restored the Bourbon monarchy in France, and took steps to control Russian attempts to gain influence in Europe. A German confederation was created to replace the Holy Roman Empire, with the aim of tamping down remaining revolutionary energy in the German states. Austria and Prussia turned themselves into police states, as an attempt to control dissent, but they were only prolonging the inevitable fall of the old monarchies.

The 1830 revolution in France influenced restless Germans and started riots there. A liberal spirit in Germany was tightly linked to an emerging nationalism, raising the level of conflict among the German people. In the spring of 1848, revolutions broke out across Europe. These were middle-class driven, most with the objective of replacing the old monarchies. Over 50 countries participated, each acting independently, with no coordination. Most revolts were put down quickly, but some lasted longer. The most important revolutions took place in France, the Netherlands, and Germany.

The German states experienced revolts starting in Baden, expanding to the Palatine, and then Prussia. In each case, surprised rulers quickly agreed to public demands for a democratic state with a new constitution. These concessions turned out to be fraudulent; the rulers reversed themselves when they realized their armies could put down the revolts. By 1851, all the initial concessions had been removed and things were back to the old way.

One of the goals of the revolution had been to create a unified German state, but that effort failed because the forces moving in that direction could not reach a consensus on what a unified Germany should look like. An assembly, put together by the member states to design a new government, had no power and could not influence the direction of the country. Germany was not yet ready for unification.

The Age of Bismarck
The Age of Otto Von Bismarck began when he was selected, by the King of Prussia to be the Minster President and Foreign Minister of Prussia in 1862. Bismarck had worked his way up the Prussian political ladder, starting as an assemblyman in 1849. In 1851, he was named to the Diet of the German Confederation and his eight years in that body convinced him German unification had to be pursued. Bismarck was named Ambassador to Russia in 1857, but

returned to Prussia in 1862 to help resolve a constitutional crisis. Beginning that year, he successfully managed the political affairs of the Prussian government, although he was disliked by members of the other parties.

In 1866, Bismarck made up an excuse to declare war on Austria. The war was over in seven weeks and the German Confederation, which had included Austria, was dissolved forever. Bismarck's next move was war with France, undertaken to subdue Prussia's other principal enemy. After a six-month campaign, the French surrendered, and Germany was free to resolve its internal problems. Nationalist emotions released during the war made the German unification process a likely prospect, so Bismarck negotiated with representatives of the southern German states and offered special concessions if they agreed to his plan. The negotiations succeeded and patriotic sentiment overwhelmed the remaining opposition.

Bismarck's balance of power approach helped maintain peace in Europe during the last decades of the 19th Century. This "Revolutionary Conservatism" was a Conservative state-building strategy designed to make ordinary Germans more loyal to state and emperor, through the creation of a modern welfare state. His strategy was to grant social rights to enhance the integration of a hierarchical society and forge a bond between workers and the state. That bond would strengthen workers, maintain traditional relations of authority between status groups, and provide a check against the forces of Liberalism and Socialism. This balancing act of political interests allowed the traditional conservative elements to retain control of the country while accommodating liberal interests with welfare programs. Bismarck became a hero to German Conservatives, who erected monuments to him after he left office in 1890.

After Bismarck

After Bismarck, German Conservatism became "Volkish," (nationalistic). Between 1890 and the end of the First World War, nationalist ideas caused the merging of the German Liberal Party with the Conservatives, expressing a common affinity toward nationalism. In a few years, the Catholic Party would join the coalition. When the First World War ended, Conservatives adopted a "pre-Fascist" stance, positioning themselves against the working class. That development replaced the old "Volkish" faction with a more modern version of nationalism. A new party, the German National People's Party (DNVP), advanced the Conservative banner and replaced the old Fatherland party. The DNVP was eventually replaced by the Nazi Party and was forced out of existence until the end of World War II, when it was revived

After the war, changes in Central Europe forced a fundamental re-evaluation of German Conservatism. By the early 1950s, the Conservative vote had begun to concentrate around a single, large, popular party that appealed to the masses by not being exclusively Conservative. German Conservatism's traditional division had been Catholic and Protestant, but now a party called the German Democratic Union (GDU), used its strong Catholic base to consolidate former Centre Party supporters, Protestant Christian

Socialists, old guard Conservatives, German Nationalists, and Volkisch nationalist moderates into a composite electoral whole. The result was an amalgamated Conservative Party with a wide range of political views.

More recently, the work of Conservative CDU leader and Chancellor Helmut Kohl (1930-2017) helped bring about German Reunification, along with the closer integration of Europe in the form of the Maastricht Treaty. Today, German Conservatism is often associated with politicians such as Angela Merkel (1954-), whose tenure (2005-) has been marked by attempts to save the Euro from demise. The German Conservatives are divided under Merkel due to the refugee crisis in Germany. Many Conservatives oppose the refugee policies she has implemented.

Points to Remember

1. Political Conservatism emerged during the period when England moved from a strong monarchy to a parliamentary form of government in the late 17th Century.

2. The first great Conservative thinker was Edmund Burke, who stressed the importance of using time-tested institutions as a brake against change-driven, radical political ideas.

3. The English Tory Party originally favored the monarchy over the people, but eventually pivoted toward Democracy and became Britain's modern Conservative Party.

4. Germany evolved during the 19th Century from a group of separate states to a unified republic. This transition was engineered by Otto Von Bismarck, who defeated Austria and France, before unifying the German nation. Working from a conservative position, Bismarck constructed a welfare state system, which kept German politics stable for a generation.

CHAPTER SIX

THE AMERICAN CONSERVATIVE MOVEMENT TO 1955

What is conservatism? Is it not the adherence to the old and tried against the new and untried?

Abraham Lincoln

Prior to 1955, there was no Conservative ideology in America. Traditional Conservatives were a faction of the people who settled the American Colonies, and they carried forward the typical characteristics of resistance to change and a preference for the status quo. These Conservatives brought old world traditions with them to serve as a foundation for Colonial society. These old-world traditions served as a foundation for Conservatism in Colonial society.

Conservatives were not involved in politics until 1854, when the Republican Party was formed. From that point forward, they applied their beliefs to the new party's platform and used it to oppose liberal ideas.

Between 1955 and 1980, a Conservative ideology emerged and became a force in American politics. By the time Ronald Reagan was elected in 1980, the Republican Party and the Conservative ideology had reached their zenith. Then, during the Reagan years, Conservatives became complacent, while the Left, using academia and the media, began to take over the culture narrative. By 2000, Conservatives had forgotten the intellectual rigor they had used in the past. The Republican Party was fractured and no longer operated as a unified organization.

The Colonial Period

Before an ideology existed, conservative was the label applied to Americans who resisted change and supported traditional values and views. In Colonial America, the first Conservatives opposed independence and supported the Crown. They stood against the Enlightenment Liberalism of colonists who wanted to break from the English system. Many of the Founding Fathers took a middle position, labelling the creation of an American government as a continuation of the government of England, which resulted when the Glorious Revolution of 1688 stripped away the power of the monarchy and replaced it with a democracy.

John Adams believed history had shown the importance of aristocrats in a political system. Since ancient times, the intelligent, well-educated, and most experienced individuals had been trusted to control governments, based on their skills and commitment to the good of society. By contrast, middle- or lower-class individuals were distrusted as more likely to give up their commitments to society for monetary gain. Adams believed men differed in temperament and ability, so their pursuit of success rendered inequality inevitable. Adams' observation and assessment of the French Revolution validated his concerns about making changes to a political system solely to achieve equality. The French Revolution showed how an idealistic search for an unreachable goal had ruined a great nation for almost a century. This case gave support to the view that governments should limit power granted to the people.

After the Constitution was enacted and the new government put into operation, the Federalist faction assumed the role of conservatives. They viewed the Democratic-Republicans of Jefferson as misguided for believing in the wisdom of the common man. The Federalists thought of themselves as the keepers of an established order, believing they were acting as a British Constitutional government without a king.

Despite their efforts to dominate the government of the new republic, the Federalists could see that the people of the United States wanted their country to be more democratic, based the on political gains made by Jefferson's party. The people's will and desire to be free of an aristocratic model was just too strong to resist, reflecting the independent nature of the American people.

The 1790s was a turbulent decade as the horror of the French Revolution unfolded and Napoleon proved the point that revolution in the name of the people would lead to tyranny. In the United States, the feud between the political factions reached its peak in 1798. America was close to war with France because of that country's attacks on American ships, so President Adams sent envoys to France to negotiate a treaty that would prevent armed conflict. Hamilton, acting as an advisor to the president, advocated aggressive measures against France, while, at the same time, Jefferson's Democratic-Republicans were sympathetic to the French and criticized the Federalists for being too friendly with the British. As negotiations dragged on, Congress funded an expansion of the American Navy to protect its merchant fleet.

After the first round of negotiations failed, Adams kept secret the outrageous treatment the French had meted out to the American negotiators; he feared, if those facts were revealed, it would lead to war with France. Congress demanded the release of the documents pertaining to the negotiations and there was a firestorm when they became public. Congress asked for a declaration of war from the president, but Adams refused.

Continuing tension between the political factions over foreign policy drove the Federalists to pass the four Alien and Sedition Acts in 1798. These acts were designed to prevent foreign actors from plotting against the interests of the United States and to prosecute Americans who made false statements critical of the American government. The Federalists' excuse for passing these laws was fear of treasonous elements at work in the United States, but the Democratic-Republicans believed that enacting the new laws was solely intended to stifle dissent coming from them. All those accused and tried in Federal courts under the new law were Democratic-Republicans, and many were sent to prison.

The election of 1800 saw the first significant philosophical shift in American politics since its government was established 11 years earlier. Thomas Jefferson was elected president, representing the Democratic-Republican Party, and the Federalists were now relegated to the role of critics of the new president's programs. For a generation, they exercised that role and then passed out of existence.

In 1814, a group of northern Federalists, upset with repeated election losses, and with the direction they saw the country moving, decided it was time to secede from the union. Fortunately, their discussions came to nothing; the incident turned out to be the last gasp of a dying party. Federalist dreams were shattered by the people's acceptance of an expanding democracy and the that belief all white men were equal. Support for an aristocratic ruling class had disappeared.

Andrew Jackson
Conservatism in the United States changed its character after the election of Andrew Jackson (1767-1845) as President in 1828. He led the new Democratic Party (the former Democratic-Republicans of Jefferson) which was dedicated to carrying on the agrarian model of Jefferson. This model viewed the ideal American as a southern plantation owner. Jackson fought with Congress repeatedly, and appeared to be the tyrant the old Federalists and Southern Conservatives had worried about. The Jacksonian Democrats were against any concentration of power and saw economic growth as a precursor to that possibility. To them, rapid changes in American democracy would tear down or destabilize the

republic. Fortunately, America passed peacefully through the Jacksonian period, while Europe experienced a series of revolutions that created havoc through the first half of the 19th Century.

Conservative reaction against Jackson produced the Whig Party, which opposed everything he stood for. Whig heroes Daniel Webster and Henry Clay beat the drums for a moderate conservative path linking the past and future. That path would encourage social stability, economic modernization, and specialization. The Whigs feared both Jackson's "mass democracy" and the absolutism of the abolitionists, who were just beginning to make themselves heard.

Lincoln and Conservatism
The rise of Abraham Lincoln and the advent of the Republican Party occurred in tandem. The party was built on a combination of political views that made sense when combined into a single party platform. There was no Conservative ideology yet, because no intellectual rigor had been applied to building a framework for conservative ideas.

Before the Republican Party came into existence, Lincoln considered himself a member of the Whig Party. The Whig philosophy contained many principles that Republicans would eventually embrace, including an interventionist economic system supporting tariffs, federal government support of new infrastructure, and a national bank. The Whigs also supported modernization, meritocracy, and the rule of law. Their primary support came from entrepreneurs, planters, reformers, Protestants, and the emerging urban middle class, who found the new party's principles attractive.

The Whig Party was undone, nevertheless, by increasing controversy over slavery. In 1854, Democratic Senator Stephen Douglas (1813-1861) of Illinois, pushed the Kansas-Nebraska Act through Congress, which allowed voters in the new territories of Kansas and Nebraska to decide whether slavery would be permitted within each of their borders. This new law negated the Missouri Compromise of 1820, which banned slavery north of Latitude 36 degrees 30 minutes, the southern border of Missouri. The 1820 compromise was intended to keep the number of slave and free states equal.

Now, old wounds of the slavery controversy were reopened because the South could expand the number of slave states north of the previous line. Widespread protests began across the country and the law was opposed by some Democrats. One of the most strident groups opposing the law were the "Know Nothings," a fringe party who kept their beliefs concealed. Their name emerged because when asked what they stood for they would say, "We know nothing." In reality, the Know Nothings were bigots, opposed to foreigners and Catholics.

In the election of 1854, Anti-Kansas-Nebraska Law candidates, including the Know Nothings and independent Democrats, performed well, while the Whigs were beaten soundly. The poor showing of the Whigs signaled their death as a political party. A new party, called Republican, rose up from a combination of Anti-Kansas-Nebraska Act politicians, ex-Whigs, Know Nothings, renegade Democrats, and abolitionists. This was a time of high tribalism over the issue of slavery, when merely expressing one's beliefs in the wrong crowd could lead to a sound beating.

In the spring of 1855, Lincoln ran for an Illinois Senate seat and was defeated in a close election. Afterward he admitted, "I think I am a Whig; but others say the Whigs are dead and I am an abolitionist. I now do no more than oppose the extension of slavery."[12] In 1856, Lincoln attended a Republican Party organizing convention in Bloomington, Illinois, where speeches were given, denouncing slavery. Lincoln was asked to take the platform and speak. He spoke for an hour and a half about the critical importance of keeping slavery out of Kansas. He told the audience that if slavery came to Kansas, brothers would soon be fighting brothers, asserting that The South must understand that the Union must be preserved.

Lincoln was nominated for president in 1860 and defeated three other candidates to win the office. The Republican platform's focus on slavery meant that civil war was inevitable. Lincoln believed upholding the Union was necessary to maintain a conservative tradition, but he also understood that the American government would have to change in order to realize the original objectives of the Constitution.

---

[12] Lincoln, "Letter to Joshua."

The Civil War and Lincoln

The outset of the Civil War presented the ultimate conservative paradox. The Conservative South fought to protect its economic heritage, which included slavery. The Conservative North fought to preserve the Union. It was a war of Conservatives fighting Conservatives. In the North, Abraham Lincoln was desperate to hold the Union together. He used his Gettysburg Address in 1863 to reach back to the Declaration of Independence as a sanctified tradition that needed to be preserved. Lincoln also believed the Constitution had to stand for the entire nation. He did not view the war as a crusade against evil, he believed that both sides carried some guilt, and the overarching objective of the war was to bring the country back together as quickly as possible.

In the South there was a different brand of Conservatism that focused on preserving the Southern way of life. Efforts to block slavery in the new territories made Southerners realize their political leverage would steadily decrease as the country grew larger. The alternative, born out of desperation, was to leave the Union. Secession amounted to a rejection of the American Constitution in favor of a political model consistent with the Southern way of life.

During the war, the South attempted to govern itself as a loose confederation, consistent with its focus on the sovereignty of state's rights. That model failed for the same reason the Articles of Confederation failed in 1777. The Confederate system had no executive branch and no method of achieving consensus. Arguments over how to conduct the war, including central control of the military and agricultural production, were never resolved, so the South was unable to fight efficiently.

Reconstruction

When the war ended, the leaders in the South had to adjust to a new reality. First, the slave ownership model was outlawed, causing the South's economic system to collapse. Second, their quest for state sovereignty over the dictates of the federal government was overruled. Left with no good options, the South responded to their new reality by inventing a mythology around their unique history, casting their way of life as a noble endeavor thwarted by evil doers from the North. After the last of the Northern troops departed in 1877, Southern "lost cause" Conservatives began rebuilding the South to their own liking. They instituted segregation laws and attempted to build on traditional principles of racial deference. That action, taken from their remorse, meant they would develop programs to mitigate the circumstances of blacks rather than helping blacks pursue society's normal path upward. The end result of this effort was a backward-looking, unequal society, where whites defined the suffering they felt in Biblical terms. Like Jesus, their suffering would eventually lead to redemption, they believed.

Exploitation and the Progressive Movement

The period after the Civil War in the mid- 19th Century, saw the rapid growth of industrialization in the United States. As industry expanded, it began to exploit the American worker. The Progressive Movement emerged as a reaction and sought to attack political corruption and worker exploitation as evil and immoral.

The Progressives started their work in the mid-1870s and continued their fight for the American worker until World War I. During this period, Conservatives were divided into three factions. The Social Darwinists felt the need to defend the industrialists against the Progressives. They asserted the American worker must submit to a "survival of the fittest" reality. Those who were able to survive and prosper had earned their positions. Those who failed were not good enough to compete. Second were the elitists and advocates of high culture. They feared government by the wealthy, by demagogues, and by social revolution from below. They hated the entire political system, considering it ugly and corrupt.

Theodore Roosevelt (1858-1919) exemplified a third type. Like some of his peers, Roosevelt feared government by the wealthy, so he focused his energy on the era's great industrialists whom he considered greedy. Roosevelt sought a balance between the free market and government curbs on big business. Each of these three groups would eventually agree that rising Socialism and Communism represented the greatest threats to Capitalism and democracy.

The Republican Party 1854-1912
The issue of slavery dominated Republican politics from the time the party was created until the end of Reconstruction. Before the Civil War, Republicans fought to exclude the western territories from slavery. During the war they fought

to preserve the union. After the war they worked to impose the new reality of black citizenship on the South, working to achieve the goal of equal rights for all.

By 1880, with the issues of the Civil War receding into the background, the Republican Party returned to a more conventional platform. Its political planks included tariff protection, expanding the nation's infrastructure, and support for a strong federal government that would enforce the Constitution. The Republican platform for 1884 was progressive and called for regulation of the railroads, support for an eight-hour work day, civil service reform, and the creation of a bureau of labor. More of the same was offered up in 1888 when the platform featured a repeal of taxes on tobacco, support for the use of gold and silver as currency, and support of pensions for veterans.

The Republican platform of 1892 was similar to the Democratic platform in many respects, including support for constructing a canal in Nicaragua (later Panama), bi-metallic currency backed by gold and silver, and sympathy for Ireland's struggle for home rule. The platform also expressed clear support for protective tariffs and sympathy for Prohibition efforts. A foreign policy plank reaffirmed the Monroe Doctrine and achievement of the "manifest destiny" of the Republic, which meant expansion throughout the American continents.

The election of 1896 was historic because of the so called "party flip" in which the Republicans and Democrats flipped on specific issues. The Pietistic faction, a religious lobby, strongly supporting prohibition and Sunday Blue Laws, moved from the Republican to the Democratic side. The Liturgicals, who represented the traditional Christian denominations, moved from the Democratic to the Republican side. Up to that point in history, the Democratic Party had focused more on supporting Capitalism than lining up behind social issues. Now, the Republicans became a party of tariffs and moderate statism. The other important outcome of the 1896 election was a significant drop in voter turnout, which was 20% less than the prior election. A large percentage of the drop came from the poor who stopped voting, perhaps because they felt neither party represented their interests.

The Republican platform of 1900 lauded the accomplishments of President McKinley, crediting him with improving business conditions and winning the Spanish-American War in 1898. Other planks in the platform defended post-Spanish-American War expansionism; called for the creation of a Department of Commerce; condemned Southern laws designed to keep African-Americans from the polls; supported raising the age limit for child labor, and favored the construction of a canal in Panama. The 1904 Republican platform favored the protective tariff and increases in foreign trade. It also advocated for the gold standard, sought expansion of the Merchant Marine, and supported strengthening the United States Navy.

Highlights of the 1908 Republican platform included greater protections for railroad and government employees through enactment of employer liability laws; safety statutes designed to make railroads safer; shorter work hours; compensation to injured workers, and establishment of an eight-hour work day for government construction employees. The party also demanded equal justice for all and enforcement of the 13th, 14th and 15th Amendments to the Constitution, which, respectively, banned slavery, defined citizenship, and prohibited governments from denying the right to vote based on race. By 1912, equal rights for women had become a separate plank in the Republican Party platform, influenced by Progressive Party efforts during that period. The Republican platform also called for a stronger national defense and the conservation of natural resources. It condemned the Wilson administration for interference in Mexico and for its lack of involvement in the Philippines.

Over the first six decades of its existence, Republican Party platforms were driven by a combination of special interests that were many times unconnected to Conservatism. It wasn't until the 1950s that a strong link was built between Conservatism and the Republican Party. That linkage developed from an evolving Conservative Ideology that could be used to develop a winning party platform.

The 1920s and 1930s
Two important events marked a change in the direction of Conservatives in the 1920s and 1930s: World War I (1914-1918) and the Russian Revolution (1917). After the war ended, a political battle developed over whether the United States should play a permanent role in world politics. A commitment to this role was written in the terms of the Versailles Treaty, which was negotiated at the end of the

war. Senate Conservatives, led by Henry Cabot Lodge, rejected that commitment and refused to ratify the treaty.

The Bolshevik victory refocused the attention of Conservatives onto foreign policy, replacing their concerns about the recent war. Prior to 1917, America was seen as the world's revolutionary leader, building the first new nation in 1000 years out of an unsettled land rich in natural resources. Now, Russia was the world's counter-revolutionary force, attempting to expand Socialism across the globe. Conservative politics would need to evolve in order to meet this new threat. As the 1920s unfolded, a conservative reaction took hold in the United States. It promoted cultural and political elitism and renewed doubts about democracy. A wave of Nativism swept across the country, and was taken to an extreme by a resurgent Ku Klux Klan.

The 1930s introduced new shocks, beginning with the stock market crash in 1929, which precipitated the Great Depression. Franklin Roosevelt (1882-1945) defeated Herbert Hoover (1874-1964) in the 1932 presidential election, when Hoover was blamed for the stock market crash. Roosevelt quickly began his "New Deal" program of expanding government, in an attempt to pull the country out of the Depression. Conservative reaction, led by Hoover, criticized this unwarranted growth of the Federal Government at the expense of state's rights. Hoover claimed Roosevelt was abandoning a classic liberal form of government by pursuing the opposite: a welfare state designed to take away citizens' rights in an effort to control their lives. Hoover warned Americans that Roosevelt was pursuing an unwanted concentration of power, which did not differ markedly from what Hitler was doing in Germany. Hoover railed against Roosevelt's attempts to pack the Supreme Court and rejoiced when the president's efforts were thwarted.

In the 1930s, Robert Taft (1889-1953), son of President William Howard Taft, and a senator from Ohio, became leader if the Republican Party. Taft believed in limited government and the free market. He agreed with Hoover that the New Deal was alien to the American tradition and was philosophically similar to the European dictatorships. Taft asserted that a centrally controlled economy placed impossible demands on those running the government even if they were selfless and dedicated. He further stated the New Deal "was... absolutely contrary to the whole American theory on which the country was founded, and which made it the most prosperous country in the world."[13]

During this period, a Spanish writer, Jose Ortega y Gassat (1883-1955), published *Revolt of the Masses* (1930) in which he viewed with alarm the growing influence of the masses of men and women who did not understand their world, spent their time thoughtlessly enjoying it, and did not care to excel. These undisciplined masses were degrading culture and transforming the structure of Europe by replacing the aristocracies that had historically provided leadership and discipline. They demoralized old regimes, making them vulnerable to dictatorial revolutions.

---

[13] Wunderlin. "The Papers of Robert Taft."

There were some in the United States who took the opposite position and saw the stock market crash and New Deal prescription as indications that Capitalism was a failure. Consequently, they wondered whether the cases of Italy and Germany had proved authoritarian regimes could work. They saw these systems as militant forms of Anti-Communism, or perhaps a revival of the old guild system. In either case, strong national pride was evident as these countries began to escape the Depression. Ross Hoffman (1902-79), a scholar of Edmund Burke, wondered whether America's Anti-Authoritarian bent had created too much democracy and ruined the American political system. Maybe it was time to be more authoritarian.

Embracing a variety of positions, Isolationists hung on until December 7, 1941, the day of the Pearl Harbor attack. Some felt Europe's problems were their own to solve. Taft and Hoover, respected leaders of the Republican Party, wanted the country to remain neutral, as it had many times in the past. Taft further asserted the United States at war would give Roosevelt license to complete his quest to turn the country into a dictatorship. Although sympathetic to Europe's plight, it seemed better to let Europe fall than for the United States to become a dictatorship while supporting it. By the time the war ended, the world had transformed politically, economically, and socially. Right-wing collectivism died with the Nazi regime and its genocide showed how the corruption of National Socialism could destroy a society.

In the post-WWII United States, a Conservative ideology began to evolve. Its appearance was based on the mutual interests of three groups: Libertarians, Traditional Conservatives, and Anti-Communists. Originally in separate orbits, pursuing their own objectives, these groups would unite for a common purpose in response to pressure from Liberal Democrats and the hard work of William F. Buckley.

The Rise of Libertarianism

In 1945, the United States was rapidly forced to transition from a hot war participant to a Cold War antagonist. America had allied itself with the Soviet Union in the fight against Nazi Germany and now, with the enemy eliminated, America would have to face its old partner as a competitor in the Nuclear Age. America had been transformed; business was booming, high paying jobs were available, and women were starting to become a larger part of the work force. In spite of this success, fear that an economic depression might return remained on people's minds.

At this critical moment, a newly published book would trigger the emergence of a Conservative ideology. Fredrick Hayek's book, *The Road to Serfdom* (1944), caught fire, first in Britain and then in the United States. Alarmed about government intervention into the economies of the west, Hayek wrote this as a critique of authoritarianism and a defense of free market Capitalism. Hayek argued Fascism and Nazism were logical results of the economic collectivism that grew out of Socialism. He suggested the United States could suffer the same fate as Italy and Germany, unless it took steps to protect itself.

As difficult as it was to allow the invisible hand of the market to operate, that path was better than submitting to the power of government, according to Hayek. A Socialist society that allowed the planners to govern as they saw fit would trade freedom for equality. Life in a planned society was morally degrading and interfered with basic human needs, such as independence, self-reliance, and initiative. Loss of freedom was not worth the price. Hayek did not blame the German people for Nazism, he asserted it was the logical extension of the Socialist tendencies of the late 19th Century. He was not a Libertarian in the sense that he rejected government involvement in business, but he was strongly opposed to government control of production.

Hayek studied in Vienna with Ludwig Von Mises (1881-1973) who sought to repair the reputation of free market Capitalism as the best alternative to Marxism. Von Mises argued in his book, *Socialism* (1922), that Socialist economies can't work because only a free market can determine genuine prices.

As relations between the United States and the Soviet Union deteriorated after WWII, Hayek and Von Mises brought together like-minded scholars and intellectuals from Europe and America. They met in Switzerland for 10 days in 1947 on the topics of the double threats of Communism abroad and creeping Socialism at home. Their statement, released after the meeting, was:

> The central values of civilization are in danger. Over large stretches of the earth's

surface the essential conditions of human dignity and freedom have already disappeared. In others they are in constant menace from the development of current tendencies of policy. The positions of the individual and the voluntary group are progressively underlined by extensions of arbitrary power. Even the most precious possession of western man, freedom of thought and expression is threatened by the spread of creeds which, claiming the privilege of tolerance when in the position of minority, seek only to establish a position of power in which they can suppress and obliterate all view but their own.[14]

Two American economists attended the meeting, Milton Freedman (1912-2006) and George Stigler (1922-91). Both would later win the Nobel Prize in Economics. Both would remain a part of this group for decades. Later, this organization would be called The Mont Pelerin Society after the location in Switzerland where their meetings were held.

Other notables who joined the Libertarian camp included Murry Rothbard (1926-95), an American, and Ayn Rand (1905-82), a Russian émigré novelist who lived in New York. Rothbard looked upon government as an enemy and saw America's Cold War interventionism as unnecessary. Rand, the successful author of *The Fountainhead* (1943) and

---

[14] Mt. Pelerin Society, "Statement of Aims."

Atlas Shrugged (1957), was a Libertarian by political philosophy and friends with Von Mises and Rothbard. Rand went on to develop a new branch of philosophy called Objectivism.

Embracing Libertarianism as an economic system amounted to a return to the economic roots of the Enlightenment, and Classic Liberalism. That meant small government, encouragement of Capitalism and a disinterest in foreign policy.

Traditionalists and Liberal Cooperation
During the post-war years, traditional Conservatives were searching for a voice. They had been on the outside looking in since Roosevelt was elected in 1932. Conservative influence over American culture and politics was at a low point after World War II. A common criticism at the time was that Conservatives had nothing to offer other than resistance to change. Conservatives needed an ideology to be able to respond to that criticism.

The post-World War II period was also a difficult one for Liberals. Disillusionment and uncertainty were endemic among their ideologues. Liberals tried to use energy from their New Deal success, but the air had gone out of that balloon. They were blamed for an unsatisfactory settlement at the end of the war, problems in Asia, and their acceptance of Communists in the United States government. Arthur Schlesinger, Jr. (1917-2017), an avid Liberal, questioned whether Liberalism was grounded in reality.

To address the problem of Communists in the American government, prominent Liberals formed the Americans for Democratic Action (ADA) in 1947. One of their targets was Henry Wallace (1888-1965), former vice-president under FDR and leader of the Progressive Party. Wallace favored conciliation with the Communists, which had become unacceptable to the Liberals. The ADA and right-wing Liberals defeated Wallace and the Progressives in the 1948 landslide election, and Harry S. Truman became president.

Arthur Schlesinger published *The Vital Center* (1949), which attacked the Left as naïve for not accepting the proven fact that Communism was a failure. During that time, Liberals began to look more favorably on Conservatives. That new openness made sense because Liberals needed a healthy opposition to fight the intellectual battle over politics. After years of attacking Conservatives as "businesspeople," Liberals began to define Conservatives as people who acted like them. They even allowed Conservatives like Peter Viereck (1916-2006) and Russell Kirk (1918-94) to appear in their magazines. The Liberals in the late Forties and early Fifties were realizing they accomplished much, and had to conserve those accomplishments. Samuel Huntington (1927-2008), a political scientist from Harvard University suggested that Liberals had become the new Conservatives.

The Liberal approach to the new Conservatism was narrow and limited to making friends with the Left-wing members of the Republican Party. Those friends came from the Traditionalist faction, not the Libertarians and Anti-

Communists. Conservative intellectuals viewed this friendliness with suspicion, thinking the Liberals were embarking on a "divide and conquer" strategy. Still, this attention from the Left gave Conservative intellectuals some credibility and exposure.

Traditionalist Conservative intellectuals came to believe that linking the past using classical ideas was the best foundation for moving Conservatism forward. One of the strongest proponents of this position was Richard Weaver (1910-1963), who felt that solving society's problems required an analysis of the history of ideas. Weaver believed society took a wrong turn during the Enlightenment, when mankind became refocused on the individual at the expense of society as a whole. He believed equality was harmful to society because human stability depended on a hierarchy to maintain order.

To Liberals, Weaver was a misguided authoritarian. To Conservatives, he was a champion of tradition and liberty. To Southerners, he was a refreshing defender of an "anti-modern" South. Weaver's distain for Liberals who sanctified America's past inequality struck a chord with Conservative intellectuals. His writing attacked the growing number of modern Americans denying conservative structure and moral uprightness. Weaver came to be seen as defining America's plight and as inspiring Conservatives to find "the relationship between faith and reason for an age that does not know the meaning of faith."[15]

---

[15] Weaver. "Ideas Have Consequences."

Russell Kirk, an admirer of Weaver, wrote the Conservative classic, *The Conservative Mind* (1953), which laid out the history of conservative thought from Edmund Burke to T.S. Eliot. In following Burke, Kirk defined Conservatism as the embrace of traditions, fully compatible with constitutional republicanism and democracy. He asserted that the American Revolution was a Conservative action against royal exploitation. He also believed Conservatism was fluid, based on changes to society. That fact did not deny that there were some common elements carried through time. Conservatism was the expression of the ancient moral traditions of humanity, so true Conservatives had to respect the wisdom of their ancestors and remain dubious of wholesale changes that broke from that continuum. Kirk believed in property, a benign social hierarchy, and the need for an aristocracy.

A third traditionalist writing in the post-war period was Peter Viereck, a professor at Mount Holyoke College. Viereck, like Weaver and Kirk, argued for traditional values and the worth of the accumulated experience of our civilization. He believed Christianity was the time capsule that conserved the heritage of man, after civilization rescued man from an animal state. The role of education in modern society was to pass along that heritage to each new generation.

Anti-Communists
Anti-Communists were the third vital component of the Conservative ideology in the United States. Their most famous personality was Whittaker Chambers (1901-1961), who became world famous, in 1948, for accusing Alger Hiss

(1904-1996), a State Department official, of being a Russian spy. Chambers was an admitted Russian spy himself and had joined the Communist Party as a young man, after being seduced by its characterization as a selfless cause. Chambers saw his participation as a legitimate, world-changing mission. After hearing about Stalin's purges in the 1930s, however, Chambers was shocked into realizing Communism was nothing more than the practical corruption of an ideal. The horror of the purges was its revelation that Stalin was doing what he thought was right, making Communism fundamentally evil. As a supporter of the cause, Chambers felt he was evil by association, so he began exposing Communist spies within the United States government. The most famous example was Hiss, who was a high-ranking State Department official. Hiss, who had been a regular contact of Chambers during the 1930s, was found guilty of perjury in 1949, and sentenced to five years in prison.

McCarthyism

Anti-Communist hysteria consumed the United States for five years after the Hiss case. Joseph McCarthy (1908-1957), a Senator from Wisconsin and professed Anti-Communist, served as chairman of the Senate Committee on Government Operations starting in 1953. McCarthy used as a blueprint, previous work done by the United States House Un-American Activities Committee, which was formed after World War II to root our Communism in the American government. McCarthy produced an aggressive campaign against Communists in the United States Government culminating in the Army-McCarthy Hearings of 1953-1954. Those hearings were held to investigate the infiltration of

Communists in the United States Army. McCarthy's tactics were so vitriolic and bombastic that they caused his popularity to drop precipitously. When the final report was released in January of 1954, the results were inconclusive and McCarthy's career was destroyed.

McCarthy was a side story in the discussion of Anti-Communist Conservatives. Many other ex-Communists followed Whittaker Chambers into the Conservative Movement. The most notable in this group were Max Eastman (1883-1969), Will Herberg (1901-1977), and Frank Meyer (1909-1972). By the mid-1950s, these individuals were prepared to work with other Conservative groups to build an ideology that could compete with Liberalism in the American intellectual landscape.

Points to Remember
1. During the first 60 years of our nation's history, conservative beliefs were expressed through attempts to safeguard traditions against rapid political change.

2. In 1854, the Republican Party emerged, and expressed, for the first time a link between politics and Conservatism.

3. After Reconstruction, the Republican Party carried a weak link to Conservatism into the 20th Century, as it adapted to rapid changes in American society.

4. By the mid-20th Century, three disparate groups had found common ground as they sought to build a Conservative

ideology. These groups were Traditionalists, Libertarians, and Anti-Communists.

CHAPTER SEVEN

THE AMERICAN CONSERVATIVE MOVEMENT 1955-1980

Conservatism is not about the party, because the party is merely the shell. It is the inside - it's the filling that really means something.

Jonathan Krohn

By the mid-1950s, the American Conservativism had become a vigorous, if heterogenous, movement ready to challenge the New Deal Left. What it lacked was cohesion and an intellectual foundation that could be used to validate its actions.

Liberals viewed the developing Conservative ideology with suspicion and began a two-part attack against it. First, they asserted that the traditional Conservatives, who admired Burke were misguided because America was not Europe. Europe had grown out of a feudal society which had not existed in America's history. Liberals argued the default philosophy in the United States was Liberalism, not Conservatism. By using Burke as their model, Conservatives were merely being nostalgic.

The second line of attack focused on the Libertarians and Anti-Communists, whom the Liberals regarded as misinformed based on the psychology of their behavior. The Left labeled them frustrated, maladjusted, status-seeking, fanatical neo-populists unable to cope with the complex modern world. Liberals also characterized Conservatives, in general, as submissive, lacking in confidence, hostile, suspicious, intolerant, and fearful of change. Those criticisms laid bare the fact that Conservatives could not take on the liberal establishment from a weak ideological position. During those years, Conservatives took comfort in the fact that Liberals were spending a lot of energy criticizing them. They were becoming important enough to be noticed.

William F. Buckley

William F. Buckley (1925-2008) is credited with bringing Libertarianism, Traditionalism, and Anti-Communism together into a single Conservative ideology. That accomplishment has put all serious Conservatives in his debt. Buckley burst on the scene when he published *God and Man at Yale* (1951), an indictment of his alma mater for turning its back on God and Capitalism. Buckley accused Yale of becoming a center of economic collectivism and atheistic humanism. In addition, he argued for a stricter definition of academic freedom, one in which professors would be prohibited from expressing their own personal views unless they represented the views of society as a whole. In his second book, *McCarthy and His Enemies* (1954), Buckley defended Joe McCarthy's style and tactics, labeling them politics as usual. He argued that since the

United States was at war with Communism, tough measures were appropriate.

In 1955, Buckley launched his magazine, *The National Review*, with the purpose of bringing all conservative ideas together. He pulled in Conservative intellectuals to contribute to his magazine, including Russell Kirk and Whittaker Chambers. The only Conservative faction ignored by Buckley was the isolationists, because he did not believe the United States should ignore the rest of the world. Buckley's merging of ideologies positioned him against big government in every area except defense. His principal adversaries were American Liberalism at home and Communism abroad. Buckley's motivation represented the final maturing of public response to the power of the Conservative Gene. Conservatives of the time understood that without an ideology, Conservatives could not protect their interests in the intellectual space that forms the basis for public policy.

In 1959, Buckley wrote *Up from Liberalism*, a kind of manifesto. He attacked Liberalism as a menace because it supported big government and was an intrusion into people's lives. Buckley considered Liberalism powerful but decadent, asserting that Conservatism was on the rise. He was critical of President Eisenhower because he squandered a chance to cut back the size of government and reduce the size of the welfare state during his presidency. He was also critical of Eisenhower for accepting a peaceful coexistence with the Soviet Union.

Buckley had key intellectuals on board at *The National Review* including James Burnham (1905-1987), Frank Meyer, and L. Brent Bozell Jr. (1926-1997). Burnham was a close associate of Buckley and professor of philosophy at New York University. Originally leaning Marxist, Burnham turned away in disgust when he saw the abuses of the Soviet Union. Burnham published *The Managerial Revolution* in 1941, which analyzed the governments of the United States, Nazi Germany, and the Soviet Union. He alleged that each was governed by bureaucratic elites who operated separately from the ideologies that supported them. Those elites were awash in self-interest, even as they pretended to be working for the people they served.

Burnham saw the Soviets as relentlessly expansionist, and would not be stopped unless the Allies attacked them. He considered the efforts toward containment of the Soviet Union by Eisenhower and Truman to be ineffective. Burnham recommended the United States apply intolerable pressure against the USSR by destabilizing Communist regimes, setting up opposition governments in the Soviet satellites, and using military force where it could be effective.

Frank Meyer, like Burnham, had studied at Princeton and Oxford. A Communist organizer in the 1930s, Meyer rejected Communism at the end of World War II. In 1955, Meyer joined Buckley at *The National Review*. Meyer believed in a "fusionist" concept of Conservatism, meaning that it was important for the free market to generate wealth as an offset to the concentration of power in the federal government. That concept had to be balanced against the views of some Traditionalists, who were inclined to back authoritarian governments, stifling freedom. Meyer wrote *The Conservative Mainstream* (1969), which summed up Conservative philosophy as of the late 1960s.

The Roman Catholic Church became linked to the Conservative ideology during the 1950s through Buckley and several of his associates. Unlike the typically isolationist Protestants, Catholic Conservatives saw an affinity with European Traditionalism in the fight against Communist barbarism. That view created a conflict with Libertarians and their purely Nationalistic ideology. Catholic Conservatives reacted with dismay at the direction of the Supreme Court under Chief Justice Earl Warren in the 1950s, which they saw as moving radically away from the intentions of the founding fathers. Bozell wrote *The Warren Revolution* (1966), in which he asserted that the Warren Court was systematically reversing the founding principles of the United States Constitution.

Buckley blasted the Liberals for their arrogant self-serving approach to debating the Right. He suggested that the Liberal concept of legitimate debate was more appropriate for Communists than Conservatives. Ironically, sociologist Daniel Bell (1919-2011) and some other ardent critics of the Right would later morph into allies of the Conservatives when they became Neoconservatives.

Conservatives Search for a Tradition
On their road to ideology, conservatives felt it crucial that

they identify and describe their connection to America's past. In others words, they wanted to connect themselves to American history as a form of validation, and wondered how they would accomplish that.

In the years after World War II, Conservatives saw America as an expanding world power and linked themselves to the great political thinkers of Europe, like Edmund Burke. They discounted America's direction during that period, because they didn't like the American politics they saw after the war. Traditionalists saw a "crowd culture" with no links to the past; Libertarians saw a New Deal welfare state that looked Totalitarian, and the Anti-Communists were focused outside the country with an "America against the Communists" mindset. To Liberals, this meant the Conservatives were un-American. After the war, many Conservatives considered themselves counterrevolutionaries, fighting against New Deal Liberalism. They wondered whether a Conservative who fought for change was really Conservative.

In the mid-1950s, Liberals attempted to cut off the Conservative effort to link themselves to early America. According to them, Enlightenment Liberalism was the only American political tradition; there was no Conservative tradition whatsoever. They suggested that the only link Conservatives had to history was European Feudalism, which relegated Conservatism to an import. Further extending that liberal narrative, they asserted that by admiring Burke, Conservatives were clinging to someone whose views were foreign to American life. Burke had, in fact, denied the notion of building new governments;

criticized equality; praised hierarchy, and revered the past. Liberals further claimed that Burke would be better aligned with Jefferson and the two Roosevelts than any Conservative thinker. To Liberals, the American Revolution was a Liberal event. Once the American colonists who supported the king fled, there were no Conservatives left in the colonies.

Some Conservatives ignored these criticisms. Others looked for a rational response that would support their core beliefs. One solution was to forget politics and focus on long serving traditions. For example, the Judeo-Christian tradition was certainly a link between America and Europe that transcended arguments about political ideology, while also describing the uniquely American way of life. America was like Europe in its fabric, even if the two continents differed politically.

A second counterargument was founded on a larger scale. It held that there were time honored tenets that had been consistent through the history of human society. These include natural law, liberty, and the limited state, which Conservatives viewed as timeless. They connected these traditions to early America and turned them into resistance against government power in the name of individual freedom, private property, and the authority of the individual states. Oddly, this conservative path made them look more like Jeffersonians when one would have expected them to be more closely aligned with the Federalists. The difference, of course, was the existence of the New Deal welfare state, the system Conservatives wanted to tear down.

Chicago Economists

In the early 1950s, a Conservative economic ideology began to develop. Milton Freidman and George Stigler, professors at the University of Chicago, led this effort. Initially they focused their efforts on academic research and used that as a platform to gain credibility. Their results would later serve as building blocks of a Conservative economic ideology.

Friedman and Stigler kept their conservative connection hidden until the 1960s. Unlike Von Mises, they sought a practical validation for their theories before putting them into practice. While Von Mises and Hayek's great adversary had been Communism, Friedman's and Stigler's target was Keynesian Economics. Friedman began by dismissing Marx's theory of Capitalism, which had failed to explain reality. Marx had asserted that Capitalism was unstable and the ebb and flow of business cycles would increasingly harm the worker. Reality demonstrated the opposite; the capitalist economic engine allowed workers to move up to the middle class and to find greater prosperity.

John Maynard Keynes (1883-1946) was a more formidable challenge for the Conservatives because his philosophy was at the core of the New Deal economic strategy. Keynes believed, during times of recession, government must use debt financing to stimulate demand. Then, in times of prosperity, it could raise taxes and use the extra money to retire debt left over from those recessions.

In 1962, Freidman published *Capitalism and Freedom*, which challenged the Keynesian orthodoxy. Freidman believed there was a role for government in managing the economy but not on the same level advocated by the Keynesians. He asserted that government's role was to make rules and enforce them impartially. Doing more would harm the economy. In Freidman's view, the free market had value because it decentralized power and produced wealth that benefited all. Capitalism was not discriminatory like other systems; the price mechanism determined what a commodity would cost but not who made it or who could buy it. In arguing for the free market, Freidman used research by Stigler to show that government regulators had no ability to influence the prices charged by corporations. If they did, they would soon fall under the influence of those corporations and become their puppets. The outcome of that association would be the return to a free market.

Barry Goldwater

By the late 1950s, Conservatives were anxious to put their new ideology into action. Missing a leader since the death of Robert Taft in 1953, they became drawn to Arizona businessman and veteran Barry Goldwater (1909-1998). He was elected to the Senate in 1952 and re-elected in 1958. Goldwater was sympathetic to the Conservative ideology and opposed the Eisenhower administration's centrist domestic policy. The book, *Conscience of a Conservative* (1960), was written in Goldwater's name by Brent Bozell, one of Buckley's allies. Its publication put Goldwater on the map and led him to challenge Nixon for the nomination in 1960. After Nixon lost the general election, Goldwater became the frontrunner for the next presidential election in 1964.

Goldwater was nominated in 1964, defeating George Romney, a moderate, and Nelson Rockefeller, a Liberal Republican. Party moderates were soft in their support of Goldwater because of his vote against the Civil Rights Act of 1964. During the fall campaign, President Johnson painted Goldwater as an extremist, which precipitated his landslide defeat. Goldwater was never able to broaden his following beyond core Conservatives, because the party still lacked a mature ideology.

Despite Goldwater's defeat, Conservatives were stronger intellectually because their ideology was gaining traction. Traditional Conservatives were only one faction of a Republican Party that needed a unifying ideology. The internal gap was wide, based on the incompatibility between the restraint on man's behavior advocated by the Traditionalists, and enthusiasm for individual freedom and self-assertion practiced by the Libertarians. There was great commonality around resistance to Communism abroad, and that would be the issue to complete the Conservative ideology.

Expanding the Conservative Base
After 1964, the Democratic New Deal Coalition began to fracture. Socially Conservative white Southerners began to vote Republican. African-Americans in the South began to vote for Democratic candidates, because they believed the Republicans supported segregation. A segment of white blue-collar Northerners switched to the Republican Party over social, gender, and lifestyle issues.

When the dust settled after the Vietnam War, Republicans were the main beneficiaries of the switch. The Republican Party was not just about intellectual discourse; it had an activist element as well. Crusaders, like Phyllis Schlafly (1924-2016), helped purge the party of moderate and Liberal Republicans. In addition, organizations like The Young Americans for Freedom, and the John Birch Society helped create a culture within the Conservative movement. Conservatism was now a nationwide movement, rather than cocktail party conversation between intellectuals.

Conservatives generally opposed the Civil Rights strategy utilized by the Democrats in the 1960s. They advocated for equality, rather than affirmative action, which they viewed as reverse discrimination. They also viewed the Civil Rights Act as a federal government power grab designed as a platform for liberal points of view. Conservatives generally disapproved of the tactics of Rev. Martin Luther King, Jr., which were designed to provoke a white reaction. After King's assassination in 1968, militant black leaders, like Stokley Carmichael pushed for violence against the American government, threatening to destroy the Constitutional order. Conservatives supported the suppression of those violent groups.

Conservatives argued it was a mistake for the government to offer panaceas it could not deliver. Frank Meyer echoed the words of Booker T. Washington (1856-1915) that black accomplishments and black success would have to be achieved by black people. He advocated the elimination of the minimum wage as a tool to create more entry-level jobs for all Americans.

During that period, many former segregationist intellectuals moderated their views toward African-American rights, repudiating their former discriminatory and racist behavior. The views of Conservatives reflected their moral belief in liberty and the role of government in American society. They objected to the government employing the tactics of inequality, like affirmative action, to correct historic racial inequality.

The 1968 election included the candidacy of former Governor George Wallace (1919-1998), a militant segregationist from Alabama. Wallace was attractive to both Southern whites and Northern whites who liked his opposition to the student radicals of the day. Frank Meyer, speaking for Conservative ideologues, denied that Wallace was a Conservative, seeing him as equally threatening to Conservatives and Liberals. Conservatives considered a bigoted Southern Conservative, operating under the cover of a law-and-order platform, to be inconsistent with the goals of the Republican Party.

Foreign Policy
By the late 1960s, the Vietnam War had come under withering criticism. Conservatives agreed with the domino theory of advancing Communism, but not if it had American soldiers fighting with one hand tied behind their backs. The Libertarian faction of the Conservative movement began to distance itself from the mandatory draft, arguing that mandating participation in the military required a direct

threat to the United States, which the Vietnam Conflict clearly did not. Brent Bozell argued that the anti-war teaching of the Catholic Church took precedence over the threat of Communism.

Conservatives were also upset by the policies of Henry Kissinger (1923-), Secretary of State under Nixon. Kissinger believed America could not prevail in the Cold War, so policies advocating coexistence with Communism were the best course of action. As a group, Conservatives also opposed Nixon's overtures to China, as if the crimes of that country and treatment of its people should suddenly be forgotten.

Libertarianism
While some Conservatives disapproved of the Vietnam policy on religious grounds, the Libertarians rejected a war they considered a useless foreign venture. The isolationist tradition of the old Right had never really disappeared, so even with a powerful Anti-Communist consensus, some Conservatives began to see the very state itself as the enemy. The classic Libertarian, Murry Rothbard (1926-1995), criticized the editors of *The National Review* for exaggerating the Soviet menace to justify the arms race, heavy taxes, and an increase in state power.

Moreover, some Conservatives were attracted to the New Left during the 1960s because they distrusted a state that could advocate a costly misadventure like Vietnam. The American Right had moved from opposition to the Cold War, NATO, and intervention in Korea, to endorsing militarism as a tool to oppose the mass slavery and murder of people living in Communist states. The thinking of those on the Right had changed because of its obsessive Anti-Communism. It started when Joe McCarthy mobilized the Conservative masses in the name of Anti-Communism and continued when Buckley began to employ ex-Communists in his organization.

In 1973, Rothbard published his manifesto, *The New Liberty.* He believed that war was mass murder, conscription slavery, and taxation robbery. The book's success dovetailed with the founding of the Libertarian Party in 1972. Initially consisting of utopians and hippies, who were an obstacle to expanding into the world of mainstream Conservativism, party leaders marked time until the outliers drifted away. By 1980, Libertarians were able to command 1% of the vote in the presidential campaign.

The other push Libertarianism received came from Robert Nozik's (1938-2002), *Anarchy, State, and Utopia*, published in 1974. Nozik's book was a rebuttal to the work of Progressive thinker, John Rawls (1921-2002), who had provided a social contract theory to address inequality in the United States. Rawls had argued inequalities in wealth were inherently unfair and the state was justified in redistributing wealth. Nozik denied wealth inequality was a sign of injustice, and any government effort to redistribute wealth would be tyrannically intrusive; those on the way up would have their success interrupted and those on the way down would see their wealth driven down further. To Nozik, liberty was more important than equality.

118

Domestic Problems

The late 1960s and early 1970s was a time of great upheaval in the United States. What started as a university campus reaction to oppressive administrations turned into protests against the Vietnam War and created a counterculture movement. The initial phase began at the University of California-Berkeley in 1964, when students began to agitate against restrictions on campus protests. These protests spread across the country and became front-page news. Conservatives reacted angrily, first blaming the students but then redirecting their ire against school administrations who seemed more interested in mollifying students than controlling their institutions.

Buckley asserted that institutions of higher learning were destroying the tradition that learning and thought were to be applied to solving problems in the real world. Kirk blamed the problem on boredom caused by the attendance of too many students who did not belong at university. As the child of the Counterculture Movement, the New Left expressed its moral anger over the Vietnam War and inequality by taking action. Many Leftists moved into academic fields and brought socialist ideas to universities. They rejected Capitalism as exploitive and cruel, looking to the overthrow of the federal government as a solution to the problems of inequality and racism.

Also, at that time, a youth culture was flourishing in the United States that changed everything from clothing styles and hairstyles to music, film, and other art forms. Anyone who wasn't on board was out of touch; anyone not part of the solution was part of the problem. By 1968, Conservatives were convinced that the country might collapse from race riots, student demonstrations, and rising crime rates. Meyer suggested the country was continuing a trend that had gone on for 35 years; he viewed Liberals as surrendering to Communists abroad while dismantling the Constitution at home. Despite this gloomy outlook, the zeitgeist was about to change the political landscape.

Rise of the Neocons
The Neoconservative philosophy arose as a result of cultural. urban, racial, and educational crises of the 1960s, all of which signaled the failure of Liberal politics. It began with an intellectual foundation among conservative social science professors at major universities. That gave Conservatives a foothold in academia they had never enjoyed before. Even though the Neocons understood the concerns of the Buckley crowd regarding the tradition of stability, they were looked upon with skepticism by older Conservatives on philosophical and practical grounds. It took a long time for the two movements to come to terms with each other.

Many Neocons were alumni of the Pre-WWII Left, like Irving Kristol. In 1965, he, along with the Harvard sociologist Daniel Bell, started a publication called *The Public Interest*, with the idea of diagnosing urban problems and offering solutions for them. Many academics with government ties like Daniel Patrick Moynihan (1927-2003), Seymour Martin Lipset (1922-2006), and Nathan Glazer (1923-2019) were regular contributors to the publication. These scholars were not Conservatives and asserted their intentions to be non-ideological. Bell had argued in *The End of Ideology* (1960), that problem-solving was replacing fanatical ideologies. Gradually, these men realized the issues they addressed contained unavoidable moral elements they could not dismiss. The more they dealt with morality, the more conservative they became.

The Neocons brought a fresh approach to the study of America. They asserted that a new class had come into existence in American society and it included individuals who would benefit from the expansion of government. The new class would become the administrators of the Great Society programs of Lyndon Johnson. They would also become the teachers and professors staffing the expanding public sector educational systems. The Neocons had a different philosophy than business bureaucrats, because they had a stake in the expansion of government. Many had a humanities education from which they had learned to challenge society's capitalist focus. They represented the views of a growing adversarial culture that would eventually undermine America's traditional beliefs, standards, and institutions. Social observers identified a paradox in this thinking, but American business actively promoted these changes.

Samuel Huntington asserted that as society became more educated, it became less governable. Too many students standing up for their rights and destabilizing society was bad; fewer people being educated and less interested in the voting process was better. Neocons viewed efficient government as run by experts; they saw too much pressure from the public as unhealthy. The idea of a new class of leaders was a holdover from the Neocons' Marxist past when they looked at society in terms of two classes: those with power, and those who were controlled by them.

In 1965, Daniel Patrick Moynihan contributed to this theory by publishing what has been labeled The Moynihan Report. The actual title was, *The Negro Family: The Case for National Action*. In his view, racial equality on its own was not enough to raise up African-Americans' standing. There were other socio-psychological factors, such as broken nuclear families, that stood in the way of their advancement. Until those factors were overcome, blacks would be relegated to "have not" status.

The underclass theme was further developed by Edward Banfield (1916-1999) in *The Unheavenly City* (1970). Banfield supported Moynihan's view that it was culture, not prejudice, that made inner-city progress difficult. Banfield took issue with the Liberal position that urban problems could be solved one-by-one, insisting that the problems would not go away.

Moynihan and Banfield, among others, helped define the "law of unintended consequences." They showed how the well-intended programs of the Great Society were failing, because of dynamics which the architects of those programs had not considered. Government should not try to solve problems it doesn't understand, because it cannot anticipate how successful, or unsuccessful those programs might be. The classic example of this was the continued Aid to

Families with Dependent Children program (AFDC) which began in 1935. It provided a subsidy for each child, and support for single mothers. In practice, it gave single mothers an incentive to not marry because taking that step would end their benefits.

The Neocons were not Libertarians: they wanted government to have a role in alleviating poverty, but they also recognized there were limits to what government could accomplish. The Neocons asked why most Americans were not part of the lower class. How did citizens learn and sustain a sense of social morality? A Libertarian society could not have produced it. Totalitarianism could not have produced it. What was the answer? The Neocons asserted that "mediating institutions" were the missing link. Family, church, and voluntary associations all contributed to the development of social morality.

The existence of these mediating groups, and their disruption, had implications for social policy. In the 1960s, busing students from poorer, segregated districts to wealthier segregated districts, and vice versa, was undertaken as a way to force integration. Busing was an utter failure in some states because it disrupted mediating group relationships. It was difficult for a church to help members of its community when the lives of those members were being disrupted by the movement of their children to the other side of town. Neocons asserted that the elimination of segregation did not mean integration would be successful. They cautioned the public that those who opposed busing were not racists, they were merely trying to protect their social environments. The Neocons voiced a philosophy that was Anti-Utopian, and viewed the unpractical quest for equality as the cause of repression and intolerance.

Neocons and Foreign Policy

The Neocons of the 1970s were pragmatic about foreign policy. They believed wars were inevitable and could not be prevented, so the United States must always be prepared for war. More importantly, they believed the concept of a "good war" was real. If the outcome of going to war was a more accommodating former enemy, then war was justified. Many of the Neocons supported the Democratic view of the 1950s, namely that a strong Anti-Communist belief was fundamental to the American view of the world. They begrudgingly accepted the fact that the United States should have pulled out of Vietnam earlier, but viewed that particular conflict as an exception to their ultimate mission to implement an aggressive foreign policy. In the coming decades, Neocons would play a bigger role in American Conservatism, dominating the political Right by the 1990s.

Feminism

The Feminist Movement of the 1960s had a significant impact on the attitudes of women and their position in society. Starting with Betty Freidan's (1921-2006) book, *The Feminist Mystique* (1963), radical feminists who had grown up during the 1940s, 1950s, and 1960s went into action. One of their goals was to topple sexism and remove barriers that limited women's choices and employment compensation. They also pursued freedom of education, control of their own bodies, and career progress in a male dominated society.

That effort was unacceptable to many, who thought Feminism was misguided and would ultimately create more problems for women than it would solve. Woman like Midge Decter (1927-), wife of the Neocon stalwart Norman Podhoretz (1930-), spoke out vigorously against the Feminist Movement, calling it a belief system with a weak link to Utopian Socialism and inaccuracy about the experience of women.

The war between Feminists and Anti-Feminists came to a head with the Congressional passage of the Equal Rights Amendment (ERA) in 1972. As the Amendment worked its way through the states for ratification, it became bogged down, due to the efforts of one woman, Phyllis Schlafly (1924-2016). She organized a grass roots campaign against the ERA, marking the first time in American history that large numbers of Conservative women protested against domestic political reform. They accomplished their goal. Time expired on the ratification process before the required 38 states had passed it. Phyllis Schlafly became a Conservative icon and went on to publish *The Power of Positive Women* (1977).

Another important Feminist issue was abortion, which created its own firestorm. The Feminists' position was that only women should control their own bodies, so only they had the right to decide whether to terminate or continue a pregnancy. Conservatives were not engaged in the issue

125

initially, but then some, like Bozell, began to campaign against abortion. He organized protests against abortion clinics, which included scuffles with the police, breaking windows, and getting arrested.

Things got more intense after the Roe v Wade decision in 1973, which granted women the right to abortions and nullified laws from all 50 states that had banned the practice. The growing Conservative antagonism against abortion proceeded along two fronts: one was moral, arguing that life began at conception so a zygote, then fetus, was a human being and had a right to life from that point on. The other argument was based on an analogy with slavery, during which an entire people were denied rights because they were considered essentially non-persons. In the view of Conservatives, abortion activists were treating babies as if they didn't have the right to life.

Abortion was a difficult issue for Conservatives, because there were many abortion advocates among Republican women. Intellectuals had to tread lightly to avoid upsetting their own base, concluding that political expediency was more important than ideology.

The New Christian Right
In the late 1970s, Evangelical protestants joined pro-life Catholics in opposing abortion. They also joined campaigns against a variety of lifestyle changes that were emerging in American society. Disengaged from politics since 1920, Evangelicals sensed their goal of converting one Christian at a time could benefit from political action. A primary

spokesman for the Evangelicals, Francis Schaeffer (1912-1984), warned them that ignoring politics would turn society over to secular humanists. His warning was a reaction to the publication of books like *Civilization* (1969) by Kenneth Clark (1914-2005) and Jacob Bronowski's (1908-74) *The Ascent of Man* (1973).

All through the 1970s, Schaeffer hammered away at the theme that Evangelicals needed to take action. By 1980, more than a million legalized abortions had been performed in America, and pro-life advocates argued that marriage and the family were under attack. Schaeffer also stated that the Christian Right suffered from too much emotionalism and needed more of an intellectual foundation to counter its external threats. Schaeffer was the theoretical mind behind the creation of the Moral Majority in the late 1970s. That group put itself squarely behind Ronald Reagan, whom members regarded as the man to slow the rapid change in American sociocultural customs. Their targets included the acceptance of pre-marital and extra-marital sex, widespread recreational drug use, and increases in divorce and crime.

The 1960s and 1970s saw the maturing of the Conservative movement. *National Review* Conservatives found common ground with the Neocons on domestic policy issues. Both feared the racial upheaval and street riots that took place in Detroit and Los Angeles. Both hated the New Left with its cult of political spontaneity and youth culture. They deplored the radicalization of universities and appeasement of students. They looked at Feminism as naive to the realities of sex and gender, which differentiate men from women.

Points to Remember

1. William F. Buckley is credited with singlehandedly pulling together the intellectual talent needed to construct a Conservative ideology, starting in the 1950s.

2. The Conservative ideology was supplemented by conservative economic theory, introduced by Milton Friedman and others.

3. Barry Goldwater ran for president in 1964 as the first Conservative ideologue, but was decisively defeated by Lyndon Johnson.

4. During this period, Conservatives took on a more activist character, opposing the New Left and the Vietnam War, campaigning against the Equal Rights Amendment, protesting abortion, and opposing America's friendliness toward Communist China.

5. In the late 1960s, a stronger Conservative ideology emerged. It was partially a result of the addition of the intellectuals from Neocon faction to the Conservative camp. The Neoconservatives were former Communists who separated from the New Left.

6. The Christian Right joined the Conservatives in the late 1970s. They wanted to contribute to the effort of opposing what they saw as a degrading social structure in the United Sates.

CHAPTER EIGHT

THE AMERICAN CONSERVATIVE MOVEMENT 1980-2000

Lest conservatives be too proud, it's worth recalling that conservatism's rise was decisively enabled by liberalism's weakness.

Irving Kristol

Between 1980 and 2000, the Conservative ideology reached its peak, lost its direction, lost momentum, and became fractured. Conservatives became complacent after Ronald Reagan was elected, assuming they no longer had to work hard to maintain their power base. Many Conservatives became politicians, hoping to cash in on the Republican Party success, but they forgot their roots. The Republican Party fractured because of changes in the social climate in the United States. They refused to be flexible on social issues and they fell further behind in the culture war.

The Reagan Revolution
The year 1980 ended with Conservative euphoria over the election of Ronald Reagan. Their joy was tempered, however, by concerns about his vision of the Conservative ideology. Would Reagan be true to traditional values? Now that Conservatives were in power, they were going to have

to learn the difference between ideas and governance, however, some would not give in to that reality. R. Emmett Tyrell (1943-), editor of *The American Spectator*, criticized Neocons like Irving Kristol, for their ignorance about the way government operated, and further accused them of advocating issues that, if included in the Republican Party platform, would lose elections.

Important links between Conservative intellectuals and the party were the Conservative think tanks, like the Hoover Institution. Think tanks were tapped to apply intellectual rigor to developing strategies that would help win elections. They were underwritten by Conservative organizations, such as the Koch and Olin Foundations, which were themselves backed by wealthy Conservative contributors.

Reagan Foreign Policy
President Reagan believed that the peaceful coexistence position of his predecessor had failed, so he moved to a more aggressive position against the Soviet Union. Reagan pronounced the USSR an "evil empire," and embarked on a plan to build an American nuclear arsenal that would show the Soviets they could never defeat the United States. As soon as his position became known, it was challenged by the American Council of Catholic Bishops in its pastoral letter, *The Challenge of Peace: God's Promise and our Response* (1983). The premise of the letter was to demonstrate the inconsistency between God's love and the creation of weapons that could kill millions of people. Michael Novak, a Catholic Neoconservative, responded to the bishops with a letter titled *Moral Clarity in the Nuclear Age* (1983). Novak

insisted nuclear weapons had the opposite effect from the one suggested by the bishops, mainly that the presence of nuclear arsenals prevented war. In other words, nuclear arsenals achieved maximum effect with minimal damage.

As a group, Neoconservatives became concerned about Reagan's foreign policy direction. They formed the Committee for the Free World in 1981, which sought to pressure the president to live up to the statements he made during the campaign about aggressively opposing the Soviet Union. They did not like Reagan's shift to an arms control posture, or his wheat sales to the Soviet Union, which seemed to signal a retreat from his previous rhetoric.

Reagan's ambassador to the United Nations, Jean Kirkpatrick, a Neoconservative, created a new conception of regimes that were suitable partners for the United States. Totalitarian regimes were roundly rejected, but authoritarian regimes of the right character, which could be influenced to grant rights to their people in exchange for American support, were acceptable. An example of this was the military government of El Salvador. Reagan attempted to build a pro-American relationship with that country, while ignoring its history of human rights abuses.

New Defenders of Capitalism
In the late 1970s, new defenders of Capitalism emerged. Leading the way was Milton Friedman with his book *Free to Choose* (1980). Friedman was an unabashed proponent of Capitalism, which reflected views he had espoused since the end of World War II. Friedman made recommendations that

fit the Conservative ideology, but were too risky for politicians to try to implement. His work coincided with the Neocon pivot away from urban decay, to a focus on economics. They began with the debunking of the myths, "Capitalism leads to greed," and, "The minority is exploited by the majority and its invisible hand." Neocons used the work of the economist Arthur Laffer (1940-) to show that over taxation was not healthy for the economy. Laffer's point was that Capitalism was superior, because competition lowered product costs, which served as a counterweight to the massive expenditures of the welfare state.

The Birth of Neoliberalism

Neoliberalism emerged in the 1970s as the second incarnation of Classic Liberalism. The first incarnation was Libertarianism, which became a key pillar in the Conservative ideology after World War II. Libertarians viewed government as the enemy and wanted to restrain it. Neoliberals believed that government had an important role to play, supporting the Capitalist system and helping to protect it. Furthermore, Neoliberals looked at Capitalism as a global ideology and tailored their efforts to supporting Capitalism world-wide.

The advent of Neoliberalism was attributed to a memo written in 1971 to the United States Chamber of Commerce by Lewis Powell (1907-1998). At the time, Powell was a nominee to the United States Supreme Court. The title of the memo was, *An Attack on the American Free Enterprise System*, and it was a call to arms for the American business community to fight back against its critics. Neoliberals criticized the leftward trend of American academia and its support of the welfare state, suggesting the appropriate response was to create an offsetting force consisting of private research institutions who would stand for the value of business. Powell's document stimulated Conservative think tank activity through organizations such as the Cato Institute and The Heritage Foundation. These organizations began to support a Neoliberal ideology, which placed an emphasis on using all parts of society to support Capitalism. Government, for its part, should not interfere with business and should support its operation. Government should not create welfare state programs that caused inefficiency in the economy. Government should support globalization, which would expand American business interests around the world.

Initially, Neoliberalism showed itself in the policies of Democratic presidents. For example, President Carter deregulated the airlines in 1978, and named Paul Volker (1927-2019), an acknowledged Neoliberal, chairman of the Federal Reserve in 1979. Neoliberal ideas continued as public policy through the administrations of Reagan and G. H. W. Bush, most notably in the "supply-side economics" focus during the Reagan years. Clinton implemented Neoliberal ideas during his presidency. Obama used Clinton Neoliberals in his administration.

Neoliberalism has taken heavy criticism in recent years for the damage it has done to the American middle class. That criticism was based on two assertions: First, globalism advocated by Neoliberals disengages capital from people by advocating the movement of business capital to places where labor costs are the lowest. That position gave corporations the go ahead to relocate manufacturing outside the United States, regardless of the impact at home. The damage caused by this approach was a loss of middle-class jobs in the United States. Second, globalism supported unlimited immigration as a source of inexpensive labor. That philosophy gave American companies the incentive to employ illegal immigrants and lower cost VISA workers over American citizens.

There are legitimate concerns about the dominance of Neoliberal ideas across the globe. Organizations like the World Bank operate outside the control of any nation. That means they are not accountable to any electorate. The public has no control (legal or governmental) over their activities, so they are free to cause harm within nations.

Public concerns about the accountability of global corporations and the loss of jobs have been drivers for the rebirth of nationalism in the West. Displaced workers in the developed nations want to be protected from the impact of Neoliberalism, and see their home governments as the only effective agent to accomplish that goal.

Supreme Court Nominations
Robert Bork (1927-2012) was nominated by Ronald Reagan to the Supreme Court in 1987. Bork's controversial nomination hearings brought to the surface the bitter divide between Conservatives and their opponents. The Left mounted a sophisticated campaign against Bork, attacking his judicial philosophy and branding him an extremist.

Although many Liberal publications agreed the attacks had gone too far, Bork's nomination was rejected by the Senate. For the time being, Liberals had won the battle of ideologies.

Conservative Attacks on Academia

In the early 1980s, Conservative intellectuals faced a paradox. They saw themselves winning on the political side, but losing on the cultural side. They saw the country continuing to deteriorate socially, with each generation becoming less well-educated and less disciplined. The number of abortions per year had nearly doubled between 1973 and 1981. Homosexuality began to be accepted as normal sexual orientation.

Conservatives saw education as the battleground for defining American culture, and this was expressed in Allan Bloom's (1930-1992) book, *The Closing of the American Mind* (1987). Bloom, influenced by Leo Strauss (1899-1973), a well-known American political philosopher, despaired of the cult of openness in modern academia and its emphasis upon cultural relativism. To Bloom, evaluating every society non-judgmentally seemed like a mistake. Bloom believed it was an error to explain historical events and phenomena with reference to the use of reason established by the Enlightenment. It made more sense to look at history in the context of tradition, made up of the ideas and beliefs that had stood the test of time.

Bloom believed university curricula should not be subject to transient moods and must not be utilitarian. In his view, the faculty's job was to prepare students for their individual destiny, not to try to fit them into specific roles. Students should be taught to respect traditions and use them as a guide to reject evil in the world. Despite his best efforts, Bloom's idealism was not appealing to most university faculties, nor to the culture of academia in the United States. He was vilified by the academic establishment as out of touch and misguided in his beliefs. Critics argued Bloom's rhetoric was nothing more than traditional Conservative platitudes that had been around since the Enlightenment.

E.D. Hirsch (1928-) took a more moderate approach to criticism of academia with his book, *Cultural Literacy* (1987). Hirsch believed there was a consistent decline in American culture that was manifest in an educational system based on theories of relevance, rather than standards, and course content based on the experiences and literature of neglected and victimized groups. Hirsch was accused of elitism because he asserted that certain ideas and concepts, such as the Bible and Western literature, were so fundamental to American culture they should never be discarded.

Although Bloom and Hirsch were not Conservative ideologues, they stimulated the work of others. Charles Sykes' (1954-) *Prof-Scam* (1988) and *The Hollow Men* (1990) attacked the American collegiate tenure system, which had mutated from a protection system for free speech to one of specialist inbreeding, leaving teaching to graduate students. Peter Shaw (1918-2003) published, *War Against the Intellect* (1989), which criticized the use of victim groups as objects of study.

Perhaps the most influential of the attacks on academia came from Roger Kimball's (1953-) *Tenured Radicals* (1992). Kimball argued that political radicals in academia, having failed in their goal of overthrowing American society, had turned to a long-term strategy of cultural and political revolution achieved through the indoctrination of students. This strategy compromised the students' openness to the heritage of the Enlightenment. In a nutshell, their objective was to subvert the tradition of high culture embodied in the classics of Western art, literature, and thought. Moreover, these radicals "stifled academic freedom under a blanket of political correctness, preventing the free play of ideas on all issues related to race, gender, sexuality, disability and formal artistic standards."[16]

Some Conservative students reacted to the changes in academia by forming their own groups to oppose the Left. The most well-known example was *The Dartmouth Review*, which stood fast in support of a Conservative ideology. Following Dartmouth's lead, other Conservative groups sprang up at universities across the nation.

Reaction against the Neoconservatives
After years of opposition to cultural change, the Conservatives of the 1980s contemplated ways to adapt to the reality of a rapidly changing American culture. The old arguments resurfaced between those who sought power and those who sought ideological purity. Some contemplated moving to Washington to influence the function of

---

[16] Kimball, "Tenured Radicals."

government, others were content to do research that would strengthen the Conservative ideology,

Conservative traditionalists wanted M.E. Bradford (1934-1993) nominated to lead the National Endowment for the Humanities (NEH) when the position came open in 1981. They were opposed by Neocons like Irving Kristol, who favored one of their own, William Bennett (1943-), for the position. When Bennett was selected, it caused a permanent rift between the two groups. The Traditionalists formed their own faction of Conservatism called Southern Paleoconservatism. This term represented an effort to revert back to original Conservative principles, as opposed to the corrupted Pseudo-Liberal views of the Neocons.

Bradford viewed the United States as an essentially Conservative country. The early colonists honored the unwritten British Constitution and surrounded themselves with institutions that promoted civil stability and the rule of law. The colonists' religious feelings completed the picture of a deeply rooted Conservativism. After the American Revolution, an increasing emphasis on equality had distorted that heritage. Bradford and his fellow Conservatives wanted to limit government power and restore states' rights as envisioned by the founding fathers. Jefferson had understood that the temptations of power can corrupt anyone and so no one can be trusted to decide for others. That concept was far removed from contemporary America, with its immense federal government and activist judiciary. Power was now concentrated in a small, centralized group operating as an oligarchy. The fact that many Americans accepted the status quo was a sign of a lost tradition. In other words, Americans had traded liberty for the trappings of modern life. They had been seduced by an explosion of tools, machines, and resources designed to make life easier, like automobiles, kitchen appliances, and access to entertainment.

A second group of Paleoconservatives, following the lead of the Southern group, founded the Chronicles of Culture in 1977. It was equally skeptical of Neocons and Eastern establishment Republicans. The Chronicles group argued that the United States needed to restore the radically restrictive immigration policy it had enforced from 1920 to 1960. They had no patience for the Neocon principle that liberal democracy was for everyone and immigration did more good than harm. They accused the Neocons of being too complacent about the growth of the welfare state and ignoring the dangers it posed, including a concentration of power in the federal government and the bankrupting of the United States. This idea remains an important principle of Conservativism in the 21st Century.

Twilight of the Cold War and George H.W. Bush
When Gorbachev became communist leader of the Soviet Union in 1985, and implemented his reforms, American Conservatives split into two camps: Buckley's followers believed Gorbachev's efforts were a sham, while Neoconservatives such as Irving Kristol believed they were witnessing real change. The election of George H. Bush in 1988 marked the third consecutive presidential win for the Right. Conservatives and their think tanks and journals were

ascendant. Capitalism, which had been in retreat for most of the 20th Century, was again embraced by Conservative intellectuals. With the Soviet Union dissolved into separate states, and elimination of the need to focus on Communism, Conservatives wanted to get back to fighting the culture war.

Two groups were marginalized during this time: Libertarians and Paleoconservatives. The Libertarians had been unable to make electoral headway with their candidates because their opposition to the military-industrial complex had rendered them impotent during the Cold War. The Paleoconservatives faded away because their embrace of discarded cultural beliefs made them appear insensitive to race, which destroyed their credibility.

Foreign Policy
The dust hadn't settled from the fall of the Berlin Wall before the United States was drawn into a new foreign policy crisis: Saddam Hussain's attack and occupation of Kuwait in 1990. President Bush took his time building an alliance among America's allies as he prepared to retaliate. In late 1990 and early 1991, the United States attacked Iraqi forces in Kuwait and drove them out. Most Conservatives supported the attack and believed it was justifiable based on our alliance with Kuwait. Norman Podhoretz, the outspoken Neoconservative, compared this attack to what should have been done before World War II when Hitler attacked the Rhineland. The American response in Kuwait seemed to justify preemptive strikes if they could accomplish an important objective.

Delighted with the nearly bloodless six-month victory, Neoconservatives looked on with dismay when Bush declined to invade Iraq, suggesting he was asking for trouble in the future. As history has shown us, the willingness of the Neocons to attack Iraq would linger until the presidency of George W. Bush. Their zeal to implement their ideology became the hallmark of his presidency, and damaged Conservative interests for a generation.

The Fall of Bush I

During the 1990s, the Democrat-controlled Congress increased spending on social welfare programs. These expenditures helped lead to an economic recession which not only dogged most of Bush's term in office, but also contributed to his defeat in the 1992 Presidential election. Another contributing factor was his alliance with Congressional Democrats in 1990, to raise taxes despite his famous, "Read my lips: No new taxes," pledge. In doing so, Bush alienated many members of his Conservative and Libertarian base and lost their support.

The failure to remove Saddam after Desert Storm was perceived as a failure, despite the initial impression that the brief war was the right thing to do. Bush's unpopular stance on abortion (he shifted to pro-life) cost him many votes from moderates and he was damaged by Pat Buchanan's famous "Culture War speech," which railed against baby-murder, homosexual privilege, and Bill Clinton's draft dodging.

Bush's baggage, combined with Bill Clinton's smooth talk and centrist leanings, led to a Republican defeat in 1992.

Clinton was able to capitalize on the Congress-induced recession by telling the American public Bush's tax hike raised taxes on the middle class. That issue became a lesson to Republicans: They were vulnerable when they neglected economic Conservativism.

Supreme Court Nominations

In 1991, there was another controversial Supreme Court nomination: Clarence Thomas. Nominated to replace Thurgood Marshall, Thomas was seen as too Conservative by the Left, which mounted an attack against him. This attack included an allegation of inappropriate sexual behavior toward fellow attorney Anita Hill. In the end, despite the "he said /she said" allegations, the Senate voted Thomas onto the Supreme Court. Nominations for the High Court would become a political flashpoint from that point forward. One has only to think about the recent Kavanaugh and Coney-Barrett hearings to understand the extent of the rancor, even though it did not prevent either nominee from being elected to the High Court.

Conservatives After the Cold War

Conservatives rejoiced at the fall of Communism and decentralization of the Soviet Union but also realized the philosophical dilemma created for them. Anti-Communism was one of the three pillars of the Conservative movement, which had helped drive it forward after World War II. Would the death of Communism cause the Conservative Movement to fracture like it did in the 1930s and 1940s?

R. Emmett Tyrrell, editor of *The American Spectator*, published, *The Conservative Crack-up* (1992) in response to the confused state of the Conservative movement. Tyrrell argued that even though Conservatives had made headway in electoral politics, they had lost the battle for the American cultural narrative, which was then firmly in the hands of the Left. Michael Lind (1962-), a disillusioned ex-Conservative, wrote that the Conservative intellectual movement had become hopelessly divided between an elite intellectual minority and a vulgar populist mass. Intellectuals were trying to carry on the task of building the Conservative ideology, but that effort was diluted by Conservative political types who didn't care about theory.

Visions of The Future

Francis Fukuyama (1952-), who worked at the State Department in the 1990s, wrote an article in 1989 titled, *The End of History*, suggesting that the death of Communism meant democracy had achieved its place as the preeminent political system in the world. The West was victorious because competition had exhausted the totalitarian state. Fukuyama examined religion and nationalism as potential replacements for Communism, but rejected both as serious contenders. He asserted that religion could solve problems in the private sphere but not the public sphere, and speculated that nationalism could only be generated out of dissatisfaction with Liberal Democracies.

His view of nationalism required broad dissatisfaction with government as the trigger for nationalistic emotions. He failed to anticipate public reaction to the negative impact of Neoliberalism on segments of middle-class society.

Samuel Huntington (1927-2008) disagreed with Fukuyama and viewed the future as more challenging than the past. He asserted that conflict between civilizations based on culture would become the new menace. Ideologies were shallow but cultures were deep, so at some point, Western ideas would no longer hold sway against religious cultural traditions that were centuries old. Huntington was proved correct, after the rise of the Islamist state created a new enemy for the West. Radical Islamists saw the West as a culturally decadent and dangerous influence to their religious practice. They intended to teach the West a lesson and show the world how weak the West really was.

Religious Conservatives

As a result of financial troubles, the Moral Majority ended its run in 1989. Donations were down, partly because eight years of Ronald Reagan had allowed Right-Wing Christians to find their footing, and there was less interest in supporting it. The Moral Majority was replaced by Ralph Reed's Christian Coalition. This new group exerted little influence over Conservative political ideology but was instrumental in the successful election of some members of Congress in 1994.

Catholics became more involved in politics in the 1980s, stimulated by the writings of Richard Niehaus (1936-2009), who was shocked by the atrocities of the Vietnam War and the rise in the number of abortions. He was sympathetic to the Neocon criticism of Liberalism and wrote two influential books: *The Naked Public Square* (1984) and *The Catholic Moment* (1987). In the first book, Niehaus criticized the secularization of America, arguing that religion was a fundamental part of the American psyche, which must remain relevant. In the second book, he praised the Catholic Church for balancing reason and revelation. Niehaus was later ordained as a Catholic priest and formed a group called First Things, in an effort to align Protestants, Catholics, and Jews to address common interests. Those issues included opposition to Communism, the catastrophic moral decline of American society, AIDs, abortion, and pornography.

More Conservative Attacks on Academia
The Culture Wars flared up again in the 1990s. Roger Kimball published *The Long March* (2000), his sequel to *Tenured Radicals*, which analyzed the New Left movement of the 1960s and its impact on intellectuals who followed in the decades after. His conclusion was that the 1960s tore apart the traditional intellectual fabric of American academia. The result was the death of an adult value system, and its replacement by an adolescent view of drugs, sex, and aberrant behavior.

One of the flashpoints of the academic debate spilled over into the political arena. In 1992, a dispute arose between Liberals and Conservatives over the standards for teaching history in schools. Lynn Cheney (1941-), the wife of former vice-president Dick Cheney, who was head of the NEH, asked the National Center for History in Schools and UCLA to set new standards for teaching history. After two years of work, the study was delivered in 1994. Conservatives, including Cheney, were appalled by the document, which recommended that many important historical figures be removed from history curricula. These figures included Robert E. Lee, the Wright Brothers, and Thomas Edison. The United States Constitution wasn't even mentioned!

Criticism of the standards was based on excessive political correctness, which prevented presentation of a balanced point of view. The late Charles Krauthammer (1950-2018) stated, "The whole document strains to promote the achievements and highlight the victimization of the country's favored minorities, while straining equally to degrade the achievements and highlight the flaws of the white males who ran the country for the first two hundred years."[17] Controversy over the report led to the Senate's rejection of the standards. The committee then spent two more years making "improvements." The resulting report was criticized for an over emphasis on multiculturalism and Left-wing editorializing; once again, it was rejected. Gary Nash (1933-), the committee chairman, accused Conservatives of trying to put a happy face on a troubled American history. In his view, American history must be based on the story of oppressed groups struggling for inclusion. In spite of this controversy, the standards are still in use today.

1990s Politics
After the Clinton victory in 1992, the Republican Party made the decision to attack Clinton and what remained of the New

---

[17] Krauthammer. "Victimization is in."

Deal agenda. Newt Gingrich (1943-), a Congressman from Georgia and Speaker of the House, put together what he called Contract with America, which sought to implement Conservative principles as policy for the United States. The principles were reflected in a list of objectives intended to change government operations. The Republicans promised to bring those to a vote in the House in the first 100 days of the new Congress, if they were given a majority by the American people. The list of objectives included:

1. Requiring all laws that apply to the rest of the country also apply to Congress;

2. Selecting a major, independent auditing firm to conduct a comprehensive audit of Congress for waste, fraud or abuse;

3. Cutting the number of House committees, and cutting committee staff by one-third;

4. Limiting the terms of all committee chairs;

5. Banning the casting of proxy votes in committees;

6. Requiring committee meetings to be open to the public;

7. Requiring a three-fifths majority vote to pass a tax increase; and

8. Guaranteeing an honest accounting of
the federal budget by implementing zero
base-line budgeting.

Public response to the contract led to the election of 54 new Republican seats in the House and 9 new Republican seats in the Senate.

Gingrich drove a portion of the Contract with America through Congress, including welfare reform, balancing the federal budget, and a tax cut. His rude tactics have been criticized for fostering extreme partisanship in Congress during this period, an accusation that has merit. An unintended consequence of that partisanship was its contribution to the polarization in Congress, which continues today.

Gingrich eventually got in trouble over the government shutdowns of 1995 and 1996. He took a hard line against President Clinton, was forced to back down, and saw his reputation suffer for it. Ethics charges were filed against him in 1997 and Gingrich received a Senate reprimand. After the 1998 election resulted in loses by Republicans, Gingrich resigned from the speakership before he could be removed by the Republican caucus.

President Clinton showed great dexterity in his centrist approach to governing. With six years of Republican majorities to deal with, he had to reposition himself to achieve success. Against that background of shrewd politics, the Monica Lewinsky scandal exploded in 1998, leading to

Clinton's impeachment. Ultimately, he was acquitted by a Senate that refused to remove him from office.

The End of the 20th Century

Republicans finished the 20th Century in control of Congress but not the presidency. Their power base provided the leverage to enact Conservative initiatives, but they also mishandled a government shutdown and were overzealous against Clinton during the impeachment process. On the ideology side, Conservatives were still reacting to the collapse of the Soviet Union, which cancelled their Anti-Communist agenda. This left the Traditionalists and Libertarians to carry the Conservative ideology forward. Competition came from other Conservative groups, the Neocons and Neoliberals, who were trying to stake out positions of power within the party.

The last two decades of the 20th Century saw the Conservative ideology achieve its widest penetration. Academic influence was minimal, but Right-Wing think tanks prospered and contributed many new ideas. The election of Ronald Reagan had proved that Conservatives could have an impact on politics, as well as on the intellectual space. But there were also danger signs. The election of Reagan caused Conservatives to let their intellectual guard down. They reveled in political power and forgot how they got there. The influence of academia on American culture expanded and Conservatives did a poor job of addressing issues important to the American people.

Points to Remember

1. The last two decades of the 20th Century saw the Conservatives rise and fall. They reached their peak with the election of Ronald Reagan in 1980, but fell victim to the tribalism that began to emerge in the 1990s.

2. The collapse of the Soviet Union created a time of confusion for Conservatives because their ideology had been partially built around opposition to Communism.

3. Conservatives battled Left-leaning academia during most of the period, but failed to slow the Left's assault on tradition.

4. Neoliberalism emerged as a dominate ideology in the capitalist world. Oddly, its principles were embraced by both Conservatives and Liberals.

5. Neoconservatives dominated the Conservative ideology and were later opposed by a new faction called Paleoconservatives, who sought to return to traditional Conservative ideas.

6. The Democratic Party controlled the Oval Office in the 1990s after Bill Clinton defeated George H. W. Bush.

CHAPTER NINE

AMERICAN CONSERVATIVES IN THE 21ST CENTURY

The intellectual debility of contemporary conservatism is indicated by its silence on all important matters.

Christopher Lasch

The first two decades of the 21st Century have been frustrating for the guardians of Conservative ideology and the Republican Party. Although Republicans held the White House for 12 of those years, their president did not fulfill the ideological checklist his supporters had hoped for. Government got bigger, fiscal constraints were absent, and First Amendment rights came under threat. Conservatives will have to hope for a better result in the next decade.

The Conservative Ideology

By the beginning of the 21st Century, the Conservative ideology had broken down. The Anti-Communist faction withered away after the fall of the Soviet Union, leaving the Traditionalists, Libertarians, Neocons, and Religious Right to carry the ball forward. Each of these groups was burdened with liabilities that limited their effectiveness. The Libertarians continued to embrace a rigid ideology that held back their popularity. The Neocons held a prominent position after 9/11, and influenced George W. Bush's view of foreign policy, but were pushed off the political stage after the disastrous wars in Iraq and Afghanistan. Because of their perceived archaic social bigotry, the Religious Right was regularly attacked by the Left. The ineffectiveness of these groups left the Traditionalists on their own to carry forward the Conservative ideology.

George W. Bush

George W. Bush won the 2000 election over Al Gore by the narrowest margin in American history. Gore took criticism for the mistakes he made during the campaign, but he did win the popular vote. Bush got points for being a Texas outsider and "good old boy Conservative," allowing him to separate himself from Washington insiders. He introduced a concept called "compassionate conservatism," which supported the expansion of some government programs benefiting minorities, and softened the traditional Republican anti-big-government message.

Bush took office during the short recession that followed the "dot-com" bubble. His initial efforts were directed toward a tax cut that was passed and signed on June 7th, 2001. Three months later, the course of his administration and the country were changed forever. The Bush presidency was defined by his response to the 9/11 terrorist attacks and the resulting wars in Iraq and Afghanistan. Bush's approach was influenced by Neoconservatives, including Dick Cheney (1941-), his vice-president; Donald Rumsfeld (1932-), his Secretary of Defense; and Paul Wolfowitz (1943-), his Deputy Secretary of Defense. The Neocon ideology asserted that the internal workings of a foreign power become the business of the United States when that power worked to destabilize American interests. In the case of Iraq, the suspicion of weapons of mass destruction (WMDs) made a stronger case for an American attack. American military efforts were first directed against the Taliban in Afghanistan, based on their safe-haven for Al-Qaeda, and Al-Qaeda's responsibility for 9/11. The initial attack on Afghanistan took place on October 7, 2001, just twenty-six days after the 9/11 attacks.

The attack on Iraq itself began on March 20, 2003. After initial successes, the war became drawn out as Al-Qaeda and other terrorist groups began to flood into Iraq. The war lasted much longer than expected, claimed more American lives than anticipated, and cost more money than it should have. Anger over the war eventually reached beyond the Left to the majority of Americans, who began to see the conflicts in Iraq and Afghanistan as mini-Vietnams.

The Bush administration displayed an odd mix of ideologies: Conservative Traditionalism, modernization of the welfare state, Neoconservatism, and Progressivism. As the opposition, Liberals could not support Bush, even when his program fit their ideology. The wars ultimately proved too costly for the payback, especially in the case of Iraq when WMDs were not found. Disappointment over the war, the housing collapse of 2007, and subsequent recession, spelled death for Republican chances in 2008.

Barack Obama
Barack Obama was elected to the presidency twice, based on

his personal charisma and the inability of the Republican Party to put together a competitive message or candidate. Perhaps no Republican could have beaten Obama in 2008, given the dissatisfaction the American people felt that year. The Left had always sought a rock star president with charisma and they got one in Obama. Meanwhile, the Republicans nominated a Neocon, John McCain, in 2008, when dissatisfaction with the war was at its highest, and nominated Mitt Romney, an out-of-touch wealthy businessman, in their second attempt to defeat Obama in 2012. Obama's accomplishments followed a traditional Progressive line that included:

- the Affordable Care Act
- Wall Street Reform (Dodd-Frank)
- Ending the war in Iraq
- Repealing "Don't ask don't tell" for gays in the military

More significantly, Obama cemented the Progressive stranglehold on the culture wars by pushing forward social justice initiatives. The basis for some of these programs included blaming white people for cultural inequality. Non-whites got a pass. Muslim terrorists were not named when they were involved in terrorist attacks, because to name them would have amounted to bigotry, violating the Left's rules for political correctness. "Merry Christmas." was turned into "Happy Holidays," to avoid offending anyone who was not Christian. Secularization became the new religion in America and it was obvious that American pride and its national interests were seen as secondary to the Left's desire for a universal humanity.

Obama's main challenge was to navigate the Great Recession he inherited from Bush. The collapse of Wall Street and the housing crisis, which saw thousands of Americans lose their homes when they couldn't pay their mortgages, took extraordinary intervention on the part of the federal government. In the end, the banks and large corporations were bailed out, and the American public was abandoned.

As one might have expected, the Obama presidency did not satisfy Progressives who criticized him for not doing enough. Those criticisms were based on too much foreign intervention, letting Wall Street off the hook after the damage it did during the recession, and a lack of effort in advancing environmental and social issues.

Donald Trump
The 2016 election of Donald Trump turned American politics upside down and drove the traditional parties to distraction. Fundamentally, Trump succeeded for reasons expressed previously: holding on to the typical Republican voter, and adding men from the lower to middle income classes, who saw themselves excluded by a Democratic Party. Trump's election was no accident, as he rode a Populist strategy to victory. As shocked as the parties were about the reality of the 2016 outcome, there were clearly lessons to be learned. For most of the election cycle, Progressives linked their attacks to the personality of Trump and fooled themselves into believing that tearing him down

155

would carry them to victory. It was helpful to Trump that the Clinton campaign demonstrated enormous hubris by taking important core voting blocks for granted.

Trump is a rare breed, a "Republican" without a connection to a Conservative ideology. The reality of Trump's election shocked Republican politicians and Conservative ideologues alike. Since Trump's election, Republicans have seen accomplishments, like the tax bill, that never would have been possible under a Democratic administration. Its passage required a consensus among House and Senate Republicans, so Republicans delivered a victory for Trump, even if they had to hold their noses about his behavior while doing so. The tax bill fits the model of a traditional Republican strategy: stimulate growth in business so more jobs can be created, and give the public more money to spend. In this case, Trump's objectives were aligned with Congress. Unfortunately for Conservatives, there was little to be happy about overall. They were used to having candidates who behaved with politeness and courtesy, attributes that could never be used to describe Trump.

Effect of 21st Century Politics on the Conservative Ideology

Ideological Conservatives have been significantly impacted by 21st Century politics. Recall that their foundations after 1960 were built by Traditionalists, Libertarians, and Anti-Communists. Then in the 1970s, the Neoconservative movement began to advocate for a more aggressive approach to foreign policy. In the 1980s, the Paleoconservatives, a counter-current to the Neocons, came into being. The Paleos tried to resurrect the old Conservative ideology by purging Neocons and their aggressive foreign policy from the Conservative movement. The Neocon faction prevailed, but then withered during the George W. Bush Iraq/Afghanistan war years when the American people grew tired of war. That left the Traditionalists and the Libertarians to pick up the pieces.

The Bush, Obama, and Trump administrations have each had a different impact on Conservative ideology. Bush was a half-Conservative, at best; Obama was a Progressive; and Trump is a non-ideologue. The ideologues had to accept Bush, warts and all, because he met the minimum requirement for Conservative acceptance. Obama pushed Conservatives to the background and they broke into factions during their time in the wilderness. In the case of Trump, the ideologues had to live with a candidate who was Republican in name only, and didn't take orders from them.

Republican Factions

As the influence of Neocons was fading away, a new party faction arose, the Tea Party. Although the concept dated from the 1990s, the Tea Party took its mature form during the Great Recession in 2009, in response to Obama's program for rescuing mortgage holders who were forced into foreclosure by failed lending institutions. The focus of the Tea Party was on fiscal responsibility and it advocated for reduction of the national debt and federal budget deficit by reducing government spending. Protests to energize the public in that direction were held in various cities on February 27th, 2009, after President Obama announced plans for the federal government to bail out the insolvent mortgage holders.

In 2010, the Affordable Care Act was signed into law by President Obama, despite vigorous opposition by the Tea Party. That year saw the Tea Party members achieve their greatest success in electing candidates. They ran 129 Republican House candidates and 9 Senate candidates. Of those, 40 won House races and 5 won Senate races. The Tea Party faction was less successful in the 2012 election, winning 4 Senate races, but losing 20% of the House seats they had won in 2010. Then, in 2013, the Tea Party took a stand against extending the national debt ceiling.

The disruption caused by their position damaged their reputation and they began to fade from the American political landscape. One might think the Tea Party, with its fiscal focus, would have the support of Conservative Libertarians. They did not have that support because of the Tea Party's alignment with the Religious Right, a connection unacceptable to the Libertarians. Moreover, the Tea Party was opposed to the legalization of marijuana, which Libertarians supported.

In 2012, the Faith and Freedom Caucus was formed by Ralph Reed (1961-), merging his Christian Coalition with the Tea Party. According to its website, the Caucus was opposed to abortion, medical marijuana, and same-sex marriage. It supported limited government, lower taxes, education reform, free markets, a strong national defense, and the establishment of Israel as a sovereign state. In 2015,

158

The Freedom Caucus, also known as the House Freedom Caucus, came into existence. It was comprised of Conservative and Libertarian Republican members of the United States House of Representatives, who shared the same ideology. This group had no connection to Ralph Reed's Faith and Freedom Caucus.

On March 24, 2017, the American Health Care Act (AHCA), a House Republican bill introduced to repeal and replace the Affordable Care Act, was withdrawn by Republican House speaker Paul Ryan because it lacked the votes to pass. It failed, in large part, because of opposition from the Freedom Caucus. Two days later, President Trump publicly criticized the Caucus and other right-wing groups, such as the Club for Growth and Heritage Action, for opposing the House bill. Trump tweeted: "Democrats are smiling in D.C. the Freedom Caucus, with the help of Club for Growth and Heritage, have saved Planned Parenthood & Obamacare!" On March 30, 2017, Trump "declared war" on the Freedom Caucus, sending a tweet urging Republicans to fight them in the 2018 midterm elections if they didn't align themselves with the Trump agenda. Freedom Caucus member Justin Amash, quite vocal about the issue, responded by accusing Trump of giving in to the D.C. establishment.

Trump has since developed a closer relationship with the Caucus chair, Mark Meadows, who recently became his Chief of Staff. In April 2018, Trump described four Caucus members—Meadows, Jim Jordan, Ron DeSantis and Matt Gaetz—as "absolute warriors" for their defense of him during the Mueller investigation. In May 2019, the Freedom

Caucus officially condemned one of its founding members, the same Justin Amash, after he called for the impeachment of President Trump. Amash announced in June 2019 he had left the Caucus and did not want to be a further distraction to the group.

Many members of the Republican House caucus have been part of the much larger Republican Study Committee. That group has a more comprehensive approach to membership and includes most of the Republican caucus members. The Freedom Caucus is considered the most Right-Wing group within the House Republican Conference; it supports House candidates through its PAC, the House Freedom Fund. The majority of newly-elected House members joined the Republican Study Committee (RSC), which makes sense, given that most Republicans who run for Congress today are ideologically Conservative. The RSC seems to be the fastest growing group and has added 23 to its ranks (68% of the 197 Republicans), since 2016.

There are also other Republican factions, including the Republican Main Street Partnership (RMSP), and the Tuesday Group (TG). The RMSP was founded in 1994 and is a more moderate faction within the GOP, along with the Tuesday Group (TG). The RMSP has 74 members, and the TG is estimated to have between 40 and 50 members, but it has no official roster. The Tuesday Group is less powerful than the Freedom Caucus, in part because its members are less cohesive and less willing to withhold party support. Its members are more moderate and oppose strong Conservatism.

Republican Fragmentation

These discussions about factions of the Republican Party indicate how fragmented the party really is. The days of unified political parties are gone, and fragmentation is part of the explanation for the federal government's inability to get things done. Americans understand how divided the country is, based on the battles between the Left and the Right, but the factions within the parties complicate efforts to create a unified party approach to governing.

Trump's victory shouldn't seem all that surprising to scholars of American politics, especially those who study the Right. His win was hardly preordained, but his primary and general election triumphs fit into the trajectory of American Conservatism in recent decades, along with the way the GOP and American politics have evolved. From that perspective, both his candidacy and electoral college success were decades in the making, even if the outcome was anything but certain on Election Day 2016. Trump's win requires a rethinking of American Conservatism and a reevaluation of the trajectory of 20th Century American politics.

The Conservative movement was in trouble long before 2016, and its intellectuals have fretted about party disunity for years. During the 2008 primaries, David Frum (1960-), a Canadian-American political commentator, warned that the founding principles of American Conservatism were under attack and could fall apart. Republicans increasingly appeared divided, publicly and privately, over the Conservative movement and their party's economic, social, and foreign policy agendas.

Some party planks conflict with others. Cutting spending, as the business-minded Right wanted, hardly pleased hawks who wanted aggressive engagement in international affairs. Supportable domestic spending has been a non-starter with the Traditionalists, who desire small government.

Disunity could be seen in the divisive, crowded Republican primaries of 2008, 2012, and 2016 when the party struggled to find someone capable of winning back the base in the primaries and prevailing in the general election. Even Trump failed to win a majority of voters in early contests. He prevailed because the votes were split amongst too many candidates. He won even though he rarely labelled himself a Conservative. Trump made media headlines on the rare occasions when he did self-label, because those soundbites fed the raging debate in the press regarding his Right-Wing beliefs.

Populism

"Populism" is a word commonly used to describe a current political trend across the globe. It is not a new concept and has existed throughout the history of human society. Populism appears under specific circumstances and acts as a warning sign of problems in a political system.

Historian Michael Kazin (1948-) stated that "populist" refers to a candidate who looks at the public as one group, undivided by class, and views his or her elite opponents as self-serving. A populist seeks to mobilize the people against those elites. In other words, when government fails to meet the needs of a group or groups within society, a reaction will arise that opposes the government. That reaction is vulnerable to the skills of a populist.

Populism on the Left is different than populism on the Right. Left-Wing populists take the side of the people against an elite group or the establishment. Typically, Liberals oppose the business interests of Conservatives and insist they exploit the working class. Their energy comes from the common man opposing the elites. Right-Wing populists take the side of the common man against elites, whom they accuse of favoring special interest groups.

Trump as a Populist
Donald Trump is the first populist candidate to be elected president of the United States. He cut through the nomination process by beating back a large group of establishment candidates who couldn't respond to the populist wave. He won the election by holding the Republican base and using populist rhetoric to convince white men to vote for him. His slogan, "Make America Great Again," suggested the return to a time before both identity politics and political correctness began to degrade the American cultural narrative.

Populist movements are temporary; they are based on an emotional response that eventually burns out. These movements may or may not achieve their objectives, depending on whether the populist is able to fix the problems he or she was elected to address. As soon as the populist is elected, the parties begin chipping away at their major constituencies to try and gain their trust. This is an attempt to strengthen themselves and dimmish the influence of the populist.

Oddly, during the 2020 election campaign, the Democrats did not address their problem with white men. One suspects that the more radical elements of the Left are opposed to that effort because it would compromise their narrative that white men are the cause of America's problems. Surprisingly, the Democrats won the election without that constituency.

The White Man Constituency
In the last decade and a half, a Right-Wing populist movement emerged in America when white, middle class men became frustrated by the federal government's lack of interest in their concerns. The media commonly report that the Right's populist movement is primarily driven by blue collar workers. Its constituency, however, is much broader than that. The constituency also includes evangelical men, men over 50, men earning at least $50,000 per year, and non-college educated men.

White men in America are concerned that the other identity groups are ahead of them in line: women, African-Americans, Hispanics and Latinos, gays, and immigrants, to name a few. They see the other groups receiving attention and benefits from a government to which they have no access. In addition, the radical Left's attack on "white man's privilege" ignores the important role white men played in building the United States.

In recent decades, post-industrial societies have embraced a Neoliberal agenda of free movement of capital and labor to achieve prosperity. This view supports increased immigration as a means of adapting to changes in labor requirements. In the United States, both parties supported free trade deals, when Neoliberalism was more fashionable. These policies impacted white men, especially after the Great Recession, when the housing bust destroyed Americans' most important asset -equity in their homes. The loss of asset value and the risk of job loss due to the immigrant pool and increased automation caused a reaction among white men against the government.

Impeachment

The country has now moved on from the 2020 impeachment crisis. Impeachment emerged as a tactic when the other attempts to destroy Trump were unsuccessful. The Republican Party had no choice but to defend the president because, for the most part, having him in office was better than the alternative. The tribalist state of America required that the Republicans form a wall against attacks from the Left to protect their seats in Congress.

As strange as it may seem, tribalism helps Trump. Accusing him indirectly of incompetence also accuses his supporters of stupidity for backing him. Trump voters understand that the Democrats have spent the last four years trying to build case after case to remove him from office. The impeachment accusation was built on weak, uncorroborated evidence. Their zeal to take Trump down made Democrats, the Left, Liberals, and would-be Socialists blind to the reality of the potential impact this would eventually have on their own party's aspirations. Because Independents hold the keys to the election, public opinions about the fairness of the impeachment matter at election time.

How will the Trump presidency influence the Republican Party over the next decade? It depends on the party's ability to build a message that will address the concerns of the country's major constituencies. Factionalism on the Republican side is mirrored on the Democratic side. Tribal America is the cause of tribal parties. Only forces that lead to communication between the parties can bring them back together; most likely this communication would emerge from an outside threat to the American people as a whole.

Points to Remember

1. Conservative ideologues have experienced a difficult and frustrating period during the first two decades of the 21st Century. Eight years of Obama left them in the wilderness, and the two Republican presidents before and after Obama have not adhered to Conservative principles.

2. Republican intellectuals have struggled with a changing political landscape in the world, during this period. The fall of Communism, the rise of China, and globalism initiatives are continuing problems that must be dealt with. At home, the changing social and cultural landscape impacts long-standing traditions that Conservatives value.

3. The Republican Party has broken into factions, reflecting the steady social and cultural fragmentation of the United States.

3. Ideological confusion among Conservatives prevents the Republican Party from moving forward.

4. Trump's election as the first populist president, is a measure of the public's dissatisfaction with the federal government. It also threatens future prospects for the Republican Party.

CHAPTER TEN

CRITICISM OF AMERICAN CONSERVATISM

*A conservative is a man with two perfectly good legs who,
however, has never learned how to walk forward.*

Franklin D. Roosevelt

Conservatism, like any political ideology, is subject to criticism from those who oppose it. Those at the extreme right of the political spectrum are particularly vulnerable to disparagement, because their ideology is more rigid and their views are farther from the mainstream. Conservatives have never been good at defending their positions because, for the longest time, they had no ideology. It's hard to defend oneself and one's ideology without a consistent, coherent basis for one's belief. In addition, Conservatives think at an intuitive level, not an analytical level. Once established, their moral foundations propel gut-level, automatic responses to decision-making. The Left employs a more analytical strategy for decision-making because they are focused on, and prompted by, a different set of moral foundations.

General Criticisms of Conservatives
Criticism of Conservatives has changed over time, based on their own evolving ideology. For most of American history, their opponents ignored them as unworthy adversaries. Why

bother acknowledging an opponent who can never defeat you?

Prior to 1950, there was no Conservative ideology, per se, only a Conservative point of view, so criticisms were focused on Conservatives' resistance to change. Critics had long asserted that Conservatives possessed an inborn inclination to be negative, which was why they instinctively resisted change. To those on the Left, Conservatives were disconnected from reality because they reacted against change without understanding its benefits.

Conservatives also are criticized for taking opposite positions on the same issue at different times, for example, opposing foreign intervention during one period and supporting it during another. This is proof to critics that there is no Conservative ideology. Their argument is faulty, however, because it denies the historical foundations of Conservatism, which protect traditions, even when they change over time.

Conservatives are criticized for being reactionary, unprogressive, and feudalistic. Here, "reactionary" means opposing political or social liberalization or reform. "Unprogressive" refers to denying the necessity of "progression" when it is obvious that change is needed. "Feudalistic" refers to the desire for a society dominated by wealthy landowners. From time to time, these criticisms have been correct.

Conservatives attract criticism for opposing any commitment to a secular philosophy. They tend to be theistic, which refers to a belief in God, rather than deistic, which refers to the belief in natural gods, or agnostic, which questions whether God exists at all. Conservatives have remained religious believers, while Leftists have moved away from religion, claiming to be emancipated from the superstitions and primitive beliefs most religions advocate.

Conservatives adhere to order and the symbols that justify and sustain it. They believe in the continuity of experience; those are the patterns in history which provide clues to the future. They believe in an orthodoxy of tradition which includes moral order. Conservative morality acts as a break against anarchy and serves as an anchor that protects society from mob rule. Conservatives express distrust in unbounded human nature, which was a deep concern among America's founders. The founders sought ways to build a political system that would protect the people against too much democracy.

Although it seems immoral to the Left, Conservatives understand the necessity of inequality as a byproduct of Capitalism. They believe unequal wealth is an unfair result of the structure of advanced human society, and an important aspect of Capitalism's function-reward principle. In other words, those who work the hardest are entitled to gain the greatest benefit from their labor. Conservatives believe human beings are not guaranteed success in life, nor are all human beings capable of achieving the same level of success. Consequently, they resist efforts to "go against nature" and try to equalize society. They cite evidence of Socialist and Communist failures as proof that human beings are unable to achieve equality.

Conservatives believe in government with limited power. A political system must put restrictions on the operation of majority rule so it remains under control and supportive of a pluralistic society. Big government is a stepping stone to a planned society, so Conservatives are suspicious of welfare state trends because of their negative impact on the operation of the free market.

Conservatives are defenders of private property before they are defenders of Capitalism. Private property has been a part of human society for thousands of years, while Capitalism is a child of the Enlightenment.

Conservatives Lack an Ideology

In 1960, Frederick Hayek, the Austrian economist, criticized Conservatives for having no ideology. He recognized that Conservatism was legitimate and necessary in its role to resist political efforts for change when the value of change was unknown. Without their own ideology, however, Conservatives were destined to be dragged along a path not of their own choosing. Hayek said of Conservatives:

> When I say that the Conservative lacks principles, I do not mean to suggest that he lacks moral conviction. The typical Conservative is indeed usually a man of very strong moral convictions. What I mean is he

has no political principles which enable him to work with people whose moral values differ from his own for a political order in which both can obey their convictions.[18]

After 1960, it took a period of years for the Conservative ideology to become established, because Conservative intellectuals were too fragmented to put together a unified set of ideas they could move forward. Conservatism has always been an amalgam, based on intellectual positions that are linked as cousins, not brothers.

Criticisms of Conservatives from the Left vary, depending on which component of the Conservative ideology they choose to attack. The, "they refuse to change" criticism against Traditionalists has been constant over decades. Attacks on the Libertarian faction have always been driven by the Left's hatred of Capitalism. Liberals can't execute their welfare state ambitions without big government, and the Libertarians oppose the growth of government.

The Anti-Communists, operating within the Conservative tent, were criticized in a different way. Since Liberals were opposed to Communist expansionism themselves, they could not criticize the Anti-Communists for sharing the same beliefs. Instead, they let the former Communists take criticism from other Conservatives. The Conservative camp did not trust former Anti-Communists to be fully committed to Conservatism. They wondered if their new partners where actually Liberals in disguise.

---

[18] Hayek, "Why I am not a Conservative."

Tension Between the Party and the Ideologues

Historically, there has been tension between the political party people and the Conservative ideologues. The point of separation is the party's need to choose candidates who are electable and the ideologues desire to influence the party while staying true to their principles. Unless common ground is established between the two groups, the ideologues will not have any influence over government.

Tradition and the Selective Rejection of Rationalism

In his theory of evolution, Darwin stunned the world with ideas about the development of life forms resulting from adaptations to living on earth. Conservatives are often criticized for not accepting Darwin's findings as the truth. Forty-three percent of Republicans believe the earth's creatures have evolved over time, while 48% believe human beings have had the same form since they appeared on earth. Among Democrats and Independents, the percentages accepting evolution are in the mid- to upper sixties.[19]

Religion is a factor in human views on evolution. Because evolutionary concepts differ from Biblical teaching, there is a fundamental incompatibility; the stronger the religious beliefs, the more likely the individual will reject the theory of evolution. At every opportunity, the Left happily points out that the Conservative rejection of evolution means they reject all of science. This criticism is not correct because many religious Conservatives accept both science and religion, even when they reject evolution.

---

[19] Pew Research Center. "Public's Views on."

Conservative Self-criticism

Conservative self-criticism is as old as Conservativism itself. Traditionalists have always been strict about the size of their tent and what is required to be included in it. They only permit new groups to enter when there is significant overlap in beliefs, so groups that foster growth in moral capital are always welcomed. These groups believe in family, community, religion, and country.

The Conservative ideology that evolved after 1955 was a combination of the beliefs of different groups who often disagreed on fundamental issues but came together because Conservatism was the best ideological platform. Groups join or separate from Conservativism, depending on American political currents and changes to society. Traditionalists march on, no matter what, because their beliefs are the foundation upon which the Conservative ideology was built.

The Crash

R. Emmett Tyrell's book, *The Conservative Crack-Up* (1992), documents the Conservative drift from coherence to a state of fragmentation during the post-Reagan years. Tyrell labeled the Reagan years a great accomplishment because the mature Conservative ideology was in full operation. At the same time, those years failed to create institutions that could endure. In the latter stages of the Reagan presidency, Conservatism became popular, which meant it began to accumulate opportunists who took advantage of the times, even though they didn't understand it's principles. They were Conservatives in name only, had never read about, or accepted Conservative ideas, and were ideologically bankrupt. In those years, the Conservative success ran parallel to a growing resentment on the part of the Left toward the success Conservatives had achieved. Conservatives were no longer welcomed by the media, and the flow of former Liberals to the Neoconservative philosophy ended.

Lack of fresh recruits who could advance the Conservative ideology created a vacuum, opening the way for Liberals to move ahead unimpeded. Tyrell blamed the Neoliberals for fomenting confusion. Although they had moved away from New Age Liberalism, they never quite made it over to the Conservative side. Moreover, they became stuck in the ideological "no man's land" between Right and Left. The Neoliberals became dogmatic, asserting that anyone with a different view of the world was ignorant.

In the 1980s and 1990s, American culture became polarized because Conservatives were unable to build and support their position or propose an alternative to the ideas of the Left. Tyrell refers to the predominant cultural tone of the 1980s as *Kultursmog*, a perfect word to describe the constant broadcast through the media of an unrealistic world view. Because the Reagan years did not feature a cross-pollination of Conservative ideas into the American culture, the Kultursmog gained ascendency.

In Tyrell's view, Kultursmog denied the existence of intellectual individualism in favor of collectivism. It discarded modern thought, particularly the Enlightenment, in favor of postmodern ideas. Counter views were seen as dangerous because there was only one correct conception of the future world. Kultursmog turned Liberals into Progressives and, using clever coding, labeled Conservatives as representatives of the Klan, bigots, Anti-Semites, and Nazis.

The Conservatives' downfall in the 1980s was their failure to penetrate the story line of the Left or provide a reasonable alternative to it. Tyrell attributed this to the Conservatives' temperament. In his view, the true Conservative was private, not wishing to fight in the arena of ideas.

Loss of Coherence

As Tyrrell said, "Conservatives are temperamentally ill-suited for Political life:"

> They are too much given to the private, familiar, conventions unexamined and unchallenged. They are only slowly roused into public life. Progressive leaders long for the public life and public controversy, but not many Conservatives do. Robert Novak once remarked that Conservatives are indifferent to collegiality. It is foreign to their temperament. Typical Conservatives long for home and hearth. Problems beyond their narrow line of vision trouble them not. They derive deep satisfaction from the familiar unchanging fixtures of their country. The stars and stripes fluttering everywhere and Gilbert Stuart paintings of George Washington in every school. These

images calm the Conservatives uneasy minds. They conspire to induce the sleep that alarmed Orwell as the foundries of the Ruhr fired up to prepare Hitler's war machine.[20]

Liberals received a strong challenge from Conservatives in the 1970s because they pushed their ideas into places long sacred to the Right: family relations, school curricula, community relations, and commerce. The Left saw fit to interfere with the parent-child relationship, to legalize pornography, and to make abortion legal. These changes were implemented so quickly that Conservatives became restive and sought to enter politics. By the end of the 1980s, that angry momentum had dissipated.

Points to Remember

1. Conservatives have always been subject to criticism when they lacked an ideology.

2. Conservatives have also been attacked for their resistance to change and for clinging to tradition.

3. Starting in the 1960s, a Conservative ideology evolved, but its energy did not survive the Reagan years.

4. The Conservative ideology has often been at odds with the Republican Party because Conservatives do not usually embrace a "do anything to win" approach to elections.

---

[20] R. Emmett Tyrell, "The Conservative Crack-up."

5. Many criticisms of Conservativism are valid. Conservatives do not have the same motivation as Liberals, and are hesitant to enter the political battlefield.

CHAPTER ELEVEN

DESTROYING TRADITION, A CASE STUDY

Among the lessons taught by the French Revolution, there is no sadder and more striking than this, that you may make everything else out of the passions of man except a political system that will work.

James Russell Lowell

Of all the political upheavals in Western history, the French Revolution best demonstrates the importance of a Conservative philosophy. The French Revolution destroyed the most basic, long-lasting traditions of the French people, including their church, nobility, economy, and government. As if the French people did not suffer enough from the Revolution itself, they were forced to endure an additional 75 years of instability and economic disruption, while their country tried to establish a permanent political system. For decade after decade, the most powerful advocates for monarchy, republic, and empire competed for control. Finally, in 1870, a democratic government was stabilized.

Conservatives were at work through the roughly 100 years from the 1789 Revolution to 1870 Democracy, trying to restore traditional elements of French society. Traditionalists wanted the royalty restored to reestablish the old French way of life, but Republicans rejected the old system in favor of a democracy that would express Enlightenment values. Empire builders sought power for its own sake, thinking they knew best how France should be governed. Unfortunately, too much of the old aristocratic system had been erased during the worst years of the Revolution. Those who could have contributed to developing a logical transition had been eliminated in the waves of violence that focused vitriolic anger on all who might lead the government.

The French Revolution began for two principal reasons: Bankruptcy of the national treasury, and widespread starvation following a series of famines that reduced crop production. Those problems were exacerbated by the arrogant opulence of the monarchy, which destroyed the French people's trust in their king. Unfortunately, the revolutionary response placed power in the hands of individuals who were unqualified to manage the transition, and incapable of designing, much less implementing, a new form of government. Those who took power held narrow views and did not act in the best interests of their nation. Their efforts were driven by envy, power-seeking, and revenge.

In 1789, the population of France was 28 million people. Until 1795, France was the most populous country in Europe. In fact, it was the third most populous country in the world, behind only China and India. Demographic changes in the centuries before the Revolution had led to a massive increase in the urban population of France, although the country remained fundamentally rural. Paris was one of the most populous cities in Europe, with some 650,000 citizens by 1800. At the same time, London had just over 1 million people while the population of the United States was 5.3 million.

Economy

In the last decades of the 18th Century, French industry continued to expand. Mechanization replaced manual work and factories were created. Growth in the industrial sector was limited by competition from England in the textiles and cotton industries. Nevertheless, French commercial ventures grew both domestically and internationally. The American War of Independence led to a reduction in American trade of cotton and slaves with France, but by the 1780s, French-American trade had rebounded and was stronger than before.

Paris became France's center of international banking and investment, although Swiss banks provided the capital. The Bank of France did not exist until it was created by Napoleon in 1800. Agricultural and climatic problems of the 1770s and 1780s led to a significant increase in poverty, with some cities in the north experiencing a 20% poverty rate. Displacement and lawlessness also increased, and the rise in numbers of beggars and bandits became a problem. Economic depression impacted the wealthy and elite, but the hardest-hit were the working class and the peasants, who lost their jobs or saw their businesses fail.

Beginning of the Revolutionary Period

In 1789, France had essentially no government outside of the monarchy. There was a national parliament, but that body had no legislative power. It consisted solely of judges who managed and enforced French law across the country. As France's financial plight became more apparent to the people, they applied pressure to create a political body that could advise King Louis XVI (1754-1793) on how to address the crisis. A body for that purpose, the Estates General, had been used previously, but not since 1614.

The Estates General was made up of three constituencies: The First Estate was the clergy; The Second Estate was the nobility, and The Third Estate was the common people. After public demands for a greater say in government in November 1788, the king's privy council agreed to form a new Estates General. That assembly would be made of up 1000 members: 250 each from the clergy and the nobility, and 500 representing the common people. The king refused to accept the privy council's proclamation and sought ways to defeat it.

On May 2nd, 1789, King Louis XVI called a meeting of the Estates, to begin on May 5th. That day, he gave a speech discussing the country's budgetary problems, but offering no solution to them. He refused to recognize a need for changing the structure of the French government. Instead, the king proposed that the three Estates meet separately to elect their own delegates, hoping that would lessen the strength of the people's Estate. In response, the deputies of the Third Estate refused, occupied the main hall at Versailles, and invited the other Estates to join them. The nobles refused and the clergy were divided on how to respond to the request. This controversy was the tipping point in the runup to the revolution. The nobles and clergy, who in different circumstances would have sided with the people, moved over to the king's side to protect their own interests. Unsure how to proceed, the king became confused when his advisors made conflicting recommendations. While the king dallied, the people became emboldened, driven by starvation and the ineptness of the royal court.

On June 17th, the Third Estate, declared itself the National Assembly, the sole ruling body of France. Two days later, the clergy voted to join it. The following day, the king had the Estate's meeting hall closed and locked. At the suggestion of Dr. Joseph-Ignace Guillotin (1738-1814), the man for whom the guillotine was named, deputies to the assembly gathered at the king's indoor tennis court, where they swore not to separate until they had given France a new Constitution. This important moment in French history became known as the Tennis Court Oath.

On June 22nd, the Third Estate met in the church of St. Louis Versailles, joined by 150 deputies from the clergy and two from the nobility. The next day, the king addressed the group and told them he was invalidating their actions. Again, he urged the three Estates to meet separately. When the king retired from the assembly, he was followed by most of the clergy and the nobility, but the representatives of the common people remained in silence. After a few minutes had passed, Honore Comte de Mirabeau (1749-1791), a member of the nobility and talented orator, arose from his seat and spoke.

Gentlemen, I admit that what you have just heard might be for the welfare of the country, were it not that the presents of despotism are always dangerous. What is this insulting dictatorship? The pomp of arms, the violation of the national temple, are resorted to—to command you to be happy! Who gives this command? Your mandatary. Who makes these imperious laws for you? Your mandatary; he who should rather receive them from you, gentlemen—from us, who are invested with a political and inviolable priesthood; from us, in a word, to whom alone twenty-five millions of men are looking for certain happiness, because it is to be consented to, and given and received by all. But the liberty of your discussions is enchained; a military force surrounds the assembly! Where are the enemies of the nation? Is Catiline at our gates? I demand, investing yourselves with your dignity, with your legislative power, you enclose yourselves within the religion of your oath. It does not permit you to separate till you have formed a constitution.[21]

The grand master of the ceremonies, finding the assembly did not break up as the king requested, returned to reminded them of the king's order. "Go and tell your master," cried

---

[21] Mirabeau. "Speech."

Mirabeau, "that we are here at the command of the people, and nothing but the bayonet shall drive us hence."[22]

On June 27th, the king changed his mind and approved the combined meeting. Three days later, the assembly appointed 30 deputies to write a new constitution. On July 8th, Mirabeau demanded that French army units be removed from Paris, making way for the city to create its own militia. On July 14th, the revolutionaries stormed the Bastille prison in Paris, believing numerous prisoners were being held and tortured there. Only seven prisoners were found inside and they were liberated. The revolutionaries also confiscated a quantity of gunpowder for the new national militia to use.

Starting on July 17th, members of the nobility, sensing what was coming, made plans to leave France. On July 28th, Jacques Pierre Brissot (1754-1793) began publication of *Le Patriote Français*, an influential newspaper of the Girondins, members of the revolutionary movement. On August 27th, the assembly unveiled a document called, *The Rights of Man and of the Citizen*, which had been drafted by the Abbé Sieyès (1748-1836) and the Marquis de Lafayette (1757-1834), in consultation with Thomas Jefferson (1743-1826). On September 15th, Desmoulins published *Discours de la lanterne aux Parisiens* (The Streetlamp Address to the Parisians), a radical pamphlet justifying political violence and exalting the Parisian mob. In early November, the Breton Club was reconstituted in Paris at the Saint-Honore, a former Dominican monastery, under the name, Society of Friends of the Constitution. The Breton Club was originally

---

[22] Ibid.

a group from Brittany who had complaints against the government, but once they relocated to Paris, the club expanded and became more diverse.

In 1790, political clubs emerged as the major force behind the Revolution. The Cordeliers Club was founded on April 17th, but it eventually split into factions including the Mountain, which contained the Jacobins (formerly Breton Club) and the Girondists. These groups agreed the monarchy needed to be replaced but differed on how its replacement could be accomplished.

By June, the European powers, England, Austria, and Prussia, met to discuss how they could save the French monarchy and oppose the revolution. They also considered whether to let the monarchy fall and take advantage of the situation. In the end, they decided that saving the monarchy would help prevent revolutionary threats to themselves. That same month, the royal family attempted to escape France in disguise, but the king was recognized in Varennes and the family was forced to return to Paris. In September, the king accepted the new Constitution. On February 7th, 1792, Prussia and Austria signed a pact to invade France to restore the monarchy. War began that spring.

First Republic 1792-1804
Mayhem and murder marked the next five years. During this period, all the traditional French institutions were torn down. Church property was confiscated and sold, taking religious vows was forbidden, and a new currency was minted. The requirement that army officers be members of the nobility

was eliminated. The old judicial system was abolished and replaced by a new one. Trade unions and guilds were outlawed. All titles, honors, and privileges of the nobility were nullified. The revolutionary powers reorganized France into fifty political departments, each with representation in Paris. This centralized government model fostered a meritocracy in which the old aristocrats and new entrepreneurs had to compete against one another for jobs in the new government.

While the French government fought with itself, the French army responded to the attacks from the European powers. In late summer 1792, early victories emboldened the National Assembly to abolish the monarchy and create a republic. In August, the king was stripped of his authority and a permanent legislative body known as the Convention was put in place. Its membership included persons from all classes, elected by eligible voters of France. In this case, eligible voters meant less than 1% of the population of France.

Many professions were represented, including some shopkeepers, but the contingent of lawyers numbered 183 (24%) of the 749 members. The Convention was charged with managing the country during its transition to a new government, which would be called the First Republic. As time passed, factions within the Convention fought with each other for control, resulting in waves of violence.

On January 21st, 1793, King Louis XVI was executed for treason, marking the beginning of the

Reign of Terror. On April 6th, the Committee on Public Safety, dominated by members of the Jacobin Club, took control of the government. An insurrection on May 31st led to a September proclamation granting the speedy trial and execution of all those opposed to the revolution. Marie-Antoinette was executed on October 16th. Her only surviving child, a son, died in prison two years later. The majority of the Girondist faction was purged and they were executed in November 1793. The Reign of Terror continued until the July 28th, 1794 execution of radical Jacobin leader Robespierre (1758-1794).

In 1795, the Convention was replaced by the Directory, which became the official legislative body of the new French Republic, and its first task was to implement a new Constitution. The government featured an executive council of five members who had authority over a Parliament of elected officials. In October of that year, an uprising by royalists became a threat to the Directory but it was put down by General Napoleon Bonaparte (1769-1821). Napoleon was rewarded with the title, Commander of the French Army of the Interior. He went on to great success quelling revolutionary activities in France and fighting France's adversaries across Europe, ending with an unsuccessful campaign in Egypt in 1799.

Napoleon returned to France upon hearing that the French army had suffered defeats in Switzerland at the hands of the Russians. Recognizing an opportunity to take power, Napoleon initiated a coup d'état that overthrew the Directory on November 9th, and he was named First Consul of the new government. Napoleon controlled the French government for the next five years under the veneer of a republic. In truth, it was an authoritarian dictatorship.

First French Empire 1804-1815

In 1804, Napoleon named himself Emperor of the First French Empire. He fought a series of battles, collectively called the Napoleonic Wars, which expanded French control over a significant portion of Europe. By 1810, however, the French people had grown tired of war and the sacrifices its people were making. Military reverses, including the ill-conceived attack on Russia, caused the French army to collapse in 1814 and Napoleon was forced to abdicate. He was exiled to the island of Elba, only to escape in early 1815. He led a 100-day revolt to try and regain power, but his efforts were unsuccessful and he was exiled for the final time to St. Helena Island in the Atlantic Ocean.

Bourbon Restoration 1814-1830

After the fall of Napoleon, the European allies, including the Holy Roman Empire and England, forced France to adopt a constitutional monarchy with King Louis XVIII (1755-1824), brother of the executed king, as ruler. This was clearly a European Conservative reaction against the Revolution and its belligerent empire. The new government retained many of the changes adopted during the Revolution, including the seizure of titled land, because there was no practical way to go back to the old system.

Conservatives were bitterly split during the restoration period. The old aristocracy and the new entrepreneurs fought each other for control of the Conservative Party. Members of the old aristocracy wanted their land back and showed no loyalty to the new regime, while newcomers, including businessmen and entrepreneurs, believed the old aristocrats' time had passed. Both groups feared disorder, but their distrust of each other was greater than their fear of revolution. Unfortunately, the monarchy was inconsistent in its governance, favoring different factions at different times.

Louis XVIII died in 1824 and his brother, Charles (1757-1836), became the new monarch, Charles X. Charles was the leader of the Ultra-Royalist Party, which was farther to the Right ideologically than the government. He worked to return the rights of the former aristocracy, including compensating those from whom estates were taken. The election of 1830 produced a split government and the king dissolved Parliament. Charles' speech on the failure of the legislature ignited widespread civil unrest. By July, the monarchy had collapsed and Charles had abdicated. He named his grandson as his replacement, but the Parliament refused to grant the crown to young Henry of Bordeaux, who was only 10 years old. Instead, they named the Duke of Orleans, Louis Philippe (1773-1850), to rule as King over a government of national sovereignty.

July Monarchy 1830-1848
Louis Phillipe was placed on the throne consequent to an alliance among the people of Paris, Republicans, and middle-class businessmen. In a repeat of previous periods, Louis Phillipe's reign was marked by turmoil and dissent. From the beginning, many Conservatives, fearing their positions were threatened, demanded the old monarchy be restored. Meanwhile, Republicans and Socialists were pushing their agendas to build a new government without any link to a monarchy.

Early on, Louis Phillipe pursued an agenda that attempted to stabilize the government around *The Charter of 1830*, a modified Constitution produced through a compromise between Constitutionalists and Republicans. It removed the king's power to initiate legislation, abolished Catholicism as the state religion, and eliminated hereditary peerage. Although these changes gave the appearance of a path toward a democratic state, they were really undertaken to concentrate the power of the Conservatives. Voting rights were doubled during

Louis Phillippe's reign, expanding the vote to 200,000, but that number still represented only one percent of the French population. The net effect of the change in voting rights was to increase the number of middle-class businessmen who could vote, making them an increasingly important voting bloc against the nobility.

In October 1830, the Conservatives were purged from the government. As a result, two new parties appeared: The Movement Party and the Resistance Party. The first was a reformist party dedicated to pushing France toward a nation-state, aligning itself with other similar movements across Europe. The Resistance Party had a different objective; it wanted peaceful coexistence with the other monarchies of Europe.

The July Monarchy endured a series of traumatic events before it passed from the scene. Elections were held under changing coalitions, and the results accomplished little, if anything. Famines continued, causing riots almost every year. Those riots were punctuated by insurrections in 1831, 1832, 1834, and 1836. The unproductive Federal Government was powerless to help the country through its economic problems. In 1846, there was another famine and prices fell once more. Many of those employed in factories lost their jobs. In Roubaix, a city north of Paris, 60% of the citizens were unemployed. By 1848, the king was worn out and abdicated in favor of his grandson, Phillipe Comte de Paris, who was rejected by Parliament.

Second Republic 1848-1852
The French Republicans would not allow the Prince Philippe Comte de Paris to take control of the government. Instead, they set up an alternative government to replace the July Monarchy. Their claim was that the existing government must be replaced, having done nothing to help the poor for 60 years. Giving in to Republican demands, the government agreed to a single election in which all French citizens could vote. On May 5th, the vote was held and a new assembly was elected. The Republicans recognized immediately that the assembly was too moderate and was not close enough to a Republican system. Riots broke out in May and June.

A new Constitution, laying out a democratic republic, was demanded and the drafting of that document was completed by November 4th. A nationwide election followed on December 10th. Louis Napoleon Bonaparte, nephew of Emperor Napoleon Bonaparte and a member of the Imperialist Party, was elected. His inclination toward empire building would turn out to be another bad sign for France.

For three years the new president battled with the heterogeneous assembly which was too divided to oppose him. During that time, Louis Napoleon consolidated his power and waited for an opportunity to take control. He shrewdly played himself against the conservative and unpopular monarchists and the disorganized Republicans.

Second Empire 1852-1870

On December 2nd, 1851, Louis-Napoléon staged a coup d'état by dissolving the National Assembly and declaring himself sole ruler of France. He re-established universal suffrage as an attempt to demonstrate his openness to democracy, and a new constitution was enacted in January 1852.

The new constitution made Louis-Napoléon president for 10 years, with no restrictions on his re-election. Although it concentrated virtually all governing power in his hands, Louis-Napoléon was not content with merely being an authoritarian president. As soon as he signed the new Constitution into law, he set about restoring the empire. The Senate scheduled a second referendum in support of the empire in November and it passed with 97% support. Like the December 1851 referendum, most of the "yes" votes were fraudulent.

With dictatorial powers, Louis Napoleon placed the highest priority on building a good railway system. With Paris as a hub, he consolidated three dozen small, incomplete lines into six major companies, funding the effort through government loans. Paris grew dramatically in terms of population, industry, finance, commercial activity, and tourism. Working with Georges-Eugène Haussmann (1809-1891), Prefect of Paris, Louis Napoleon spent lavishly to rebuild the city into a world-class showpiece.

Eventually public opinion turned against the emperor. The lower classes became restless, seeing that their opportunities were next to non-existent; the business class saw a loss in profits from trade deals negotiated by the government. All were attracted to collectivist speeches touting the benefits of Communism. Louis Napoleon reacted by trying to gain the support from the Left to make up for the support he had lost from the Conservative Right. Instead, he was forced to make compromises, including a general amnesty in August 1859, which marked the country's evolution from an absolutist or authoritarian government to a liberal, and later parliamentary republic.

French overseas territories tripled in area during the next decade. By 1870, French possessions covered almost a million square kilometers, with control of nearly five million inhabitants. While soldiers, administrators, businessmen, and missionaries came and went, few Frenchmen permanently settled in the colonies, except from some in Algeria. Louis Napoleon had been successful in spreading the French culture and language outside of France.

The rise of neighboring Prussia during the 1860s threatened French influence over Western Europe, and Louis Napoleon, growing steadily weaker in body and mind, badly mishandled the politics of the situation. A Prussian prince was in line for the Spanish throne; his ascendency would have trapped France between two Prussian empires. The prince's candidacy was withdrawn under pressure from the French, but Louis Napoleon fell into a trap set by Prussian President Bismarck. The Prussian statesman released a letter to the European public in which he implied that the Prussian emissary had humiliated the negotiator from France. Six days later, France declared war on Prussia. The large French army proved to be poorly armed, poorly trained, and poorly led by the Emperor himself. In a matter of weeks, after the Battle of Sedan, the French were forced to surrender. Louis Napoleon was captured by the Prussian army. As a result of the subsequent power vacuum, Republican forces took control of Paris. Under the leadership of Léon Gambetta (1838-1882), a politician and orator, France declared the establishment of the French Third Republic.

Third Republic 1870-1940
French politics under the Third Republic were sharply polarized in the beginning. On the left stood one Conservative group, Reformist France, heir to the French Revolution. On the right stood another

Conservative group, rooted in the peasantry, the Roman Catholic Church, and the army.

Following the collapse of Louis Napoleon's regime, the French legislative election of 1871 resulted in a monarchist majority in the French National Assembly that favored a peace agreement with Prussia. The Conservatives in the National Assembly supported the candidacy of Comte de Chambord (1820-1883), a descendant of the last monarch from the senior line of the old French royal dynasty. A second Conservative faction, the Orléanists, supported a descendant of King Louis Philippe I, his grandson Louis-Philippe, Comte de Paris (1838-1894). The two Conservative factions reached a compromise whereby the childless de Chambord would be recognized as king, with the Comte de Paris designated as his heir. Chambord believed the restored monarchy had to eliminate all traces of the Revolution to restore the unity between the monarchy and the nation, but his hopes were unrealistic. The monarchists resigned themselves to wait for his death when the throne could be offered to his more liberal heir. By the time Chambord died in 1883, enthusiasm for a monarchy had faded and the Comte de Paris was never offered the French throne.

New representatives were elected in February 1871, creating the government which would evolve into the Third Republic. These representatives, predominantly Conservative republicans, enacted legislation which prompted resistance and outcry from radical and leftist elements of the republican movement. In Paris, a series of public altercations broke out between the Parisian government and the city's radical Socialists. The radicals ultimately rejected the authority of the government, responding by founding a revolutionary government called the Paris Commune.

The principles underpinning the Commune were viewed as morally unacceptable by French Conservatives who sought to maintain the tenuous, post-war stability it had established. In May, in what would become known as the Bloody Week, French Armed Forces, under the command of Patrice de MacMahon (1808-1893), marched on Paris and succeeded in dismantling the Commune.

The popularity of de MacMahon, bolstered by his response to the revolution, grew to the point that he was elected President of the Republic in May 1873. He held the office until January 1879. A staunch Catholic Conservative with royalist sympathies and a noted mistrust of secularists, de MacMahon grew increasingly at odds with the French Parliament, as liberal and secular republicans gained a legislative majority. In February 1875, a series of parliamentary acts established the constitutional laws of the new republic. A two-chamber Parliament consisting of a directly-elected Chamber of Deputies and an indirectly-elected Senate was created, along with a ministry under the President of the Council (prime minister), who answered to both the President of the Republic and the legislature. The elections of 1876 demonstrated a high degree of public support for the increasingly Anti-Monarchist direction of the Republican movement. A decisive Republican majority was elected to the Chamber of Deputies, while the monarchist majority in the Senate was maintained by only one seat.

President de MacMahon responded in May 1877, attempting to quell the Republicans' rising popularity and to limit their political influence. On May 16th, 1877, de MacMahon forced the resignation of moderate Republican prime minister Jules Simon (1814-1896) and appointed Orléanist Albert de Broglie (1821-1901) to the office. When the Chamber of Deputies expressed outrage at the appointment, believing the transition of authority was illegitimate, they refused to cooperate with either de MacMahon or de Broglie, so de MacMahon dissolved the Chamber. He then called for a new general election to be held the following October. Subsequently, both Republicans and Republican sympathizers accused de MacMahon of attempting to stage a constitutional coup d'état, a claim which he publicly denied.

The October elections again brought a Republican majority to the Chamber of Deputies, further affirming public opinion. The Republicans would go on to gain a majority in the Senate by January 1879, establishing dominance in both houses and effectively ending the potential for a monarchist restoration. President de MacMahon resigned on January 30th, 1879 and was succeeded by the moderate Jules Grévy (1807-1891). Conservatives were now pushed out of power, and the Republic was finally governed by Republicans, who supported the moderate social and political changes needed to establish a stable government. New laws were passed in 1881 and 1882 that made public education free, mandatory, and secular. These represented an important step in expanding civic powers within the Republic.

The long and arduous journey of 93 years had finally brought the French political system to the point of a sustainable government. For most of that period, Republicans seeking a new order fought with monarchists refusing to let go of the tradition of kings. This battle was continuously complicated by the Bonapartists, who wanted to see a permanent empire established. In the end, democracy won out when the institutions necessary for its survival were finally put into place.

Burke's Response to the French Revolution

Edmund Burke in his essay, *Reflections on the Revolution in France* (1790), predicted the unfortunate outcome of the Revolution. He wrote his essay as a literary letter addressed to a French friend living in France. As one of the most important Enlightenment skeptics, Burke believed in the value of traditional institutions as a guide for moving a society forward. Under no circumstances would he accept "starting over" as a method of producing good government.

He admonished his friend about what the French people had done:

> Compute your gains: see what is got by those extravagant and presumptuous speculations which have taught your leaders to despise all their predecessors, and all their contemporaries, and even to despise themselves, until the moment when they become truly despicable. By following these false lights, France has brought undisguised calamities at a higher price than any nation has purchased the most unequivocal blessings! France has bought poverty by crime! France has not sacrificed her virtue to her interest; but she has

abandoned her interest, that she might prostitute her virtue.[23]

Burke went on to explain the risk of ignoring the differences among men. Some can lead, but most cannot.

> Believe me sir, those who attempt to level, never equalize. In all Societies, consisting of various descriptions of citizens, some description must be uppermost. The levelers, therefore, only change and pervert the natural order of things.; they load the edifice of society, by setting up in the air what the solidity of the structure requires to be on the ground.[24]

Burke had great concern that the revolution in France could spill over into England so he took the time to explain to the English people how their own political system had evolved and why it was different than France.

Burke's *Reflections* received quite a bit of criticism in England, but it was also published in France and widely read. On November 17th, 1790 Burke received a letter from Francois-Louis-Thibault (1740-1816), deputy to the Estates General from

---

[23] Edmund Burke, "Reflection on the Revolution"
[24] Ibid. p. 49

Mirecourt in Lorraine. De Menonville praised *Reflections*, but asked Burke to correct some errors in the document. Burke did so in the form of a return letter sent to the National Assembly on January 25th, 1791.[25]

Conservatism in France

The history of Conservatism in France was perplexing and complicated because of that country's endless battles with itself after the Revolution of 1789. Despite the back-and-forth swings of French rule, it is truly remarkable that France was able to endure such troubles and finally achieve a stable democracy.

Joseph de Maistre (1753–1821), a strong Conservative active during the Revolution, believed the upheaval and chaos represented divine retribution for the sins of the godless Enlightenment and the "century of blasphemy" that characterized Enlightenment ideas. In his vision, one consequence of that blasphemy was the misconception involved in the creation of a written Constitution. A true Constitution could not be found in the fine words of such a document, but in the public spirit that should animate it. For de Maistre, that which was written was nothing. A Constitution was divine in origin. Only when one acted in harmony with God could their actions be creative. Once separated from the Creator, people's actions were rendered negative and destructive. The rule of number, implied by popular sovereignty, had nothing to do with the rule of justice and would ultimately prove to be self-destructive. For

---

[25] Ibid. p. 251.

Conservatives, French revolutionary history had demonstrated a succession of failed, increasingly corrupt constitutions. The disastrous history of France was as much the fault of the internal corruption of the Ancien Régime, as of the arguments of the philosophes.

De Maistre's celebrated statement, "If you wish to conserve all, consecrate all," was a proposition which he believed transformed the sacred into human life. He failed to recognize that conserving all tends to corrode the myths upon which traditions depend; it then collapses Conservatism into a unconservative reaction. The essences of Conservatism are the traditions it sanctions, which evolve and can be defended. Those traditions cannot include all because much had to be discarded. The amount discarded had to be carefully managed, to avoid the painful lesson of France.

France will always serve as a remarkable case study in the history of political systems. Its leaders could not navigate their way to a democracy once its traditions had been stripped away. The tortuous path it took caused great damage to the French people and delayed France's road to a modern nation.

Points to Remember
1. The French Revolution stands as a case study of damage that can be done by a revolution that discards a society's traditions. Any society that wants to endure must control the pace of change, so as to minimize social disruption.

2. When the French Revolution began, it came under control of those groups who did not have the best interests of their countrymen in mind, and they had no idea how to govern,

3. During the Reign of Terror, political factions fought over control of the government and there was wholesale slaughter.

4. After five years, the government stabilized, but it was weak and it collapsed when Napoleon took power as Emperor.

5. Napoleon's fall precipitated six decades of fighting for control of the country between Republicans, Monarchists, Socialists, and supporters of an empire.

CHAPTER TWELVE

THE AMERICAN CONSERVATIVE PATH FORWARD

The future of Conservatism lies in our beliefs and values, not by throwing them away. We need to shed associations that bind us to past failures, but hold faith with those things that make us Conservatives.

Iain Duncan Smith

Conservatism has evolved and developed its essential footprint through four stages in human history. The initial stage was Biological Conservatism, a functional set of inherent characteristics present in a portion of the human population. Those characteristics generated specific, useful, conservative behaviors. Biological Conservatives are careful decision-makers who opt for the status quo, rather than change for its own sake.

Stage Two was individual and collective veneration of traditions among groups in a given demographic, socio-cultural setting. As the human species developed, and man expanded his mental ability to contemplate his place in the world, traditions became important links to the past. Those traditions, which included social, cultural, and spiritual/religious components, had a stabilizing influence over human society for two reasons: They served as the bedrock for collective behavior, and they provided a normative roadmap for human progress.

Stage Three was Conservatism's connection to politics, starting in Britain after the Glorious Revolution of 1688. As the people's power increased and the power of the monarchy and the church began to diminish, political parties began to represent special interest groups. In England, members of the Tory Party were the Conservative faction. They initially misread the growing power of the people after 1688, limited themselves to protecting the monarchy, and were subsequently voted out of power for 100 years. Finally, after a century in the political wilderness, the Tories accepted the concept of a British democratic state and became the Conservative Party.

In America, there was no conservative attachment to politics until the time of Lincoln, when necessity drove the creation of a party to defend the Constitution against the South and its plan for secession. The Republican Party was formed by an amalgamation of former Democrats who opposed slavery, old Whigs who supported business, and other groups.

The Fourth and final Stage of Conservatism emerged through the development of an ideological foundation separate from the Republican Party. In the United States, in the mid-1950s, Traditionalists and Libertarians proffered their common Conservative ideology and former Communists, dissatisfied with the direction of the Democratic Party, joined them. The ideas of these groups formed the basis for a mature Conservative ideology, which expanded and eventually reached parity with Liberals during the Reagan presidency. Since 1980, the Conservative ideology has been in a state of flux, influenced by the rapid socio-cultural changes in American society. Its proponents are often at odds with the Republican Party, especially when the ideology becomes too rigid to address the practical problem of winning elections.

American Conservatives Today

The Conservative experience in the 21st Century represents a muddled picture for the future. George W. Bush was a Republican, but it is unclear whether he contributed anything to the Conservative cause. Bush embraced the Neocons, who were discredited after they fumbled the Iraq War. Obama and his party pushed a secular, global equality agenda that buried the Conservative message for eight years. Most recently, Donald Trump has operated as a Republican populist without an ideology. His administration has brought no joy to the Conservative ideologues, who saw another delay in the implementation of their ideas. These ideologues can't move forward until one of their own is in control.

Since 1994, Conservatives have accounted for 25% to 33% of the US population, based on a consensus of polls. That number contains strict ideologues who refuse to compromise their views, and more flexible Conservatives who want to get things done. The percentages have fluctuated over the past couple of decades, based on the ability of the Republican Party to address the issues important to Americans. An additional faction, making up 15% of the American population, are the moderates, who claim no party affiliation, but support some Conservative ideas. For example, they may be conservative economically, but more liberal on social issues. History shows that moderates can determine the outcome of elections, because their votes help push one of the parties over the top.

As a result of Trump's victory in 2016, the traditional Conservative ideology has been blocked from advancing. Trump was elected because his unique style and appeal harvested enough votes for him to win. Trump is no Libertarian, but his business focus, which sought to keep government from too much infringement on the free market, aligned him with basic Conservative ideas. He is a man of energy, wanting to "Make America Great Again," but also an enigma to both parties. His "America First" ideology was focused on nationalism as a counterweight to Neoliberalism, the most popular ideology of 21st Century America.

Conservatives will not be able to find their center until Trump is out of office. His persona and domination of the Republican agenda have stifled all efforts to advance the traditional Conservative ideology. Conservatives have not had a good track record of activism unless they were provoked by extreme tactics employed by the Left. The 2019 impeachment exercise was an example of Conservative anger turned into resistance. Conservatives must always find a way to aggressively fight for their positions.

Historically, Conservatives have done a poor job of countering the Left's narrative on culture, multiculturalism, and social justice, because their lack of unity has allowed the

Left to control the narrative. Conservatives are missing a unified rational message that Americans can accept and support. Trump, by contrast, appealed to people directly, using a clear message, and was not afraid to stand up to the Left. No matter what his faults may be, Trump built his popularity to a point that prevented a Conservative uprising. The recent efforts by the Never Trumpers and members of the Lincoln Project are attempts to separate true Conservatives from Trump.

What comes after Trump? A pendulum swinging back to old Conservatism? Not likely. The Neocons are defunct. Communism is nearly a non-existent factor in the West. What remains of Conservative ideology are Libertarianism and Traditionalism. Libertarianism is a cousin to Neoliberalism, an economic model embraced by many globalist Democrats. When globalism downplays the value of the state and patriotism, it separates itself from the Conservative ideology.

Another possible calamity awaiting the Republicans would be the reappearance of Trump in 2024. That specter would freeze out the retrenchment of the party and sabotage party efforts to bring an alternative candidate forward. There is no moving forward for the Republicans if Trump remains on the stage.

Conservative Libertarianism and Democracy
Conservatives will continue to push their Libertarian views into the future. This means Capitalism will continue to be an important component of Conservative ideology. There is real

momentum behind this view today because Capitalist democracies are delivering results that prove employment can "lift" people out of poverty if they choose to work.

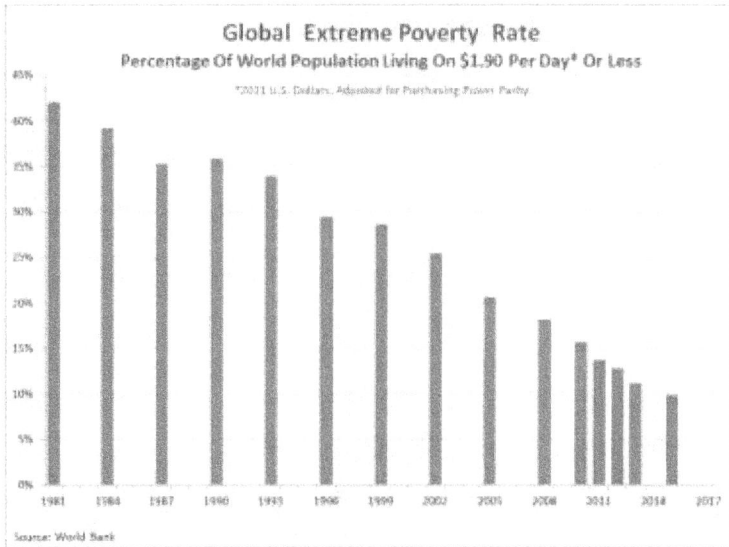

Global Extreme Poverty Rate
Percentage Of World Population Living On $1.90 Per Day* Or Less
*2011 U.S. Dollars, Adjusted for Purchasing Power Parity
Source: World Bank

The chart above depicts changes in world poverty between 1981 and 2017 and shows that a "rising tide lifts all boats." The global poverty rate was 42% in 1981 when the world population was 4.5 billion. In 2016, it was 10% with 7.4 billion inhabitants Capitalism has proved superior to all collectivist economic systems in its ability to help the world's people. Collectivist systems have never been able to demonstrate success, even within the borders of a single country.

Conservative ideology acts as a brake against collectivist support for big government and the welfare state. Collectivists cannot operate without the welfare state because implementing a Socialist political system requires a bureaucracy in which government programs are used to manage a state economy. Collectivism trades individual freedom for advancing the perceived rights of disadvantaged groups like the poor and ethnic minorities. Conservatives believe that the goals of Collectivists are utopian and impractical. The result of a Collectivist implementation of a political system is fiscal waste and ineffective service delivery.

Conservative Traditionalism
Traditionalism is the core of the Conservative belief system, reflecting the Conservatives' natural tendency to resist too much change. Most Conservatives will accept some change because they understand that change is inevitable. What they demand, though, is change within the context of tradition, because tradition moderates the speed with which politics can change society. To Conservatives, rapid change is pathological to human beings.

With few exceptions, the human race marches through time and adapts itself culturally, socially, and individually. Behaviors that were acceptable during one generation become unacceptable in the next. Likewise, behaviors that were unacceptable can reverse themselves over time. This is moral progress. Slavery was acceptable until the American people decided it was immoral. A war was fought to enforce that morality. Homosexuality was deemed unacceptable up to the 1980s, but is now considered an acceptable expression of one's sexuality. These moral changes can't be labeled good and bad, because society decides what is right and wrong.

Conservatives often have objections that are external to the gradually changing societal morality, based on universal traditions that go beyond community or nation. The best example of this involves religion. Deeply religious people take the teachings of the Bible literally, so they reject modern views of morality that are different. Their tradition is sacred and not subject to gradual change.

Today's COVID pandemic and 2020 riots provide case studies in Conservative response based on tradition. At different times during the pandemic, there have been lockdowns and curfews to limit public activity in an attempt to lower the risk of spreading the virus. Conservatives are more resistant to strict lockdowns because they interfere with liberty, meaning an individual's ability to live their life in the way they choose. They view economic shutdowns as unhealthy and economically damaging to the public, even if they decrease the COVID risk. To them, lockdowns are a cure that's worse than the disease.

The recent riots violate Conservative principles regarding the rule of law and the discarding of traditions. The rule of law is a fundamental tenet of the Constitution and forms the basis for a stable society. Without laws and law enforcement, there is only anarchy. The tearing down of statues is an attempt to erase tradition and runs counter to Conservative thinking. Discarding tradition has to be based on reason and logic, not emotion and anger.

Moral Capital

Moral Capital is a fundamental component of Conservative tradition. Originally defined by Jonathan Haidt in his book *The Righteous Mind* (2012), Moral Capital is the social morality of human beings based on kinship, association, shared beliefs, collective behaviors and events, and mutual norms and tenets.

There are four categories of Moral Capital: family, local community, moral community, and patriotism. Connections made between and among members of these groups date from when man first walked the earth until the present day. Moral Capital is the glue that holds societies together. When it is compromised, the instability in a society increases.

The Family as Moral Capital

The nuclear family is central to the continuation of the species. A man and a woman have children, raise them and protect them to continue the species into the next generation. That drive is biological. The Mom, Dad, and Children model is still the sociocultural norm, although, in recent decades, the definition of the family has changed. Same sex partners and unmarried partners are on the increase but not common. Of the 122 million households in America, 61 million are married couples, 9.7 million are cohabiting couples, and 1 million are same sex couples.[26] These structural changes do not alter the fact that the family unit of parents and children

---

[26] Pew Research Center, "The landscape of Marriage."

is the most important of the moral foundations required for the continued stability of a society.

The Social Community as Moral Capital

Local communities are groups of human beings with frequent interactions. In the primitive world, man realized working with others outside the family gave him the opportunity for a better life. Group activities such as hunting and food preparation were more productive within an amicable, cooperative group than when undertaken solely by the individual or nuclear family. Safety in numbers provided protection for families. As human society expanded, human social relationships were undertaken with caution, utilizing acquired skills to identify unproductive relationships. In the modern world, social relationships are developed in the neighborhood and the workplace by building teams or through friendships that are mutually beneficial.

The Moral Community as Moral Capital

Moral communities are groups with a deeper socio-psychological connection than an individual typically has with neighbors or co-workers. Unity is created from a shared belief system. Churches are moral communities, charities are moral communities, and even sports teams are moral communities. Membership in these groups is based on a shared belief system that is celebrated and functional. The community practices its ideology as a group, giving its members motivational energy.

Patriotism as Moral Capital

The fourth category of Moral Capital is national loyalty or patriotism, which reflect a gluing together of a society dedicated to a national goal, based on the acceptance of a common history and common experiences. The current pandemic is a test of patriotic moral capital because it impacts the entire nation and requires all Americans to unify and defend themselves against it. Unfortunately, the recent election season has stood in the way of potential unity because the strategy for fighting the disease was used as a tactic to attack Trump.

Conservatives and Moral Capital

Conservatives are the protectors of Moral Capital because they have stronger genetic foundations for Loyalty, Authority, Sanctity, and Liberty than the Left. Conservatives resist outside threats by creating strong group connections. Their biological makeup allows them to detect threats to Moral Capital that Liberals do not see.

The Left does not embrace Moral Capital per se, because its characteristics are foreign to them. As I discussed in *The Progressive Gene* (2017), the Left possesses a collectivist political morality. They think in terms of groups of people and how society treats those groups. They define special interest groups by physical characteristics rather than beliefs. The Caring and Fairness foundations of the Left drive them toward protecting the disadvantaged. They look at members of a church as members of races, rather than as a congregation of similar believers.

Liberals tend to overreach and change things too quickly, reducing the level of Moral Capital. Conservatives do a better job than Liberals and Progressives at protecting Moral Capital but fail to notice certain classes of victims, fail to limit the intentions of certain powerful interests, and fail to identify the need to change when it is important to do so. Those failures are particularly acute in the cultural space when Conservatives do not identify the need for efforts to promote equality or elevate the status of one or more groups.

Social Entropy's Attack on Human Society
Entropy is a scientific term that describes the way physical systems tend to break down into their components. In other words, systems move from an organized state to a disorganized state.

Enrique Lescure (1987-), a cognitive scientist from Sweden and cofounder of the Earth Organization for Sustainability, has utilized a term, "social entropy," to describe the behavior of Western political systems. Social entropy is a force that degrades society and increases instability. It is a natural function of human behavior, representing a tendency for humans to increase their resistance to social structure over time.

Societies consist of interacting networks of individuals and groups, so the stability of a society is supported by the rule of law, which defines the limits of acceptable behavior. Social entropy works to dissolve the institutions of a society, breaking them down into factions. Unchecked, this destructive force causes lawlessness, riots, and instability.

The United States is currently in a period of increasing social entropy with a corresponding decrease in Moral Capital. Tribalism has split the country and each tribe has been broken down further into factions that disagree with each other. The country lacks a common interest in unity because the forces of disagreement are too strong. The social unrest in 2020 reflects the failure of the rule of law and signals a temporary return to a lawless society.

On top of that, the current pandemic has impacted all the categories of Moral Capital. The family is isolated together, but forced to adopt an uncommon lifestyle, impacted by changes in employment, economic security, and children's education and care. People can't socialize because of their isolation. They can't enjoy shared beliefs through sports or their church.

The Moral Capital of our shared nationality has broken down. The tribes think of themselves as more important than the nation. This is demonstrated by the response to the pandemic, which has been wholly tribal. In normal times, the appearance of a pandemic would be a great uniter of the American people. This time, it acted as just one more divider, causing ill will and anger from each side toward the other.

Moral Ideology

As discussed previously, Conservatives possess a complex morality, created through a combination of heredity and life experience. It requires them to balance several moral foundations each time they make moral decisions. Liberty is key in their view of individual rights in society. To Conservatives, equality and liberty are diametrically opposed. A political system whose goal is to guarantee economic equality, must destroy liberty. For that reason, liberty is freedom from government oppression. Conservatives oppose the welfare state because, in their view, it gets funded by the immoral taking of their assets which restricts their liberty.

Peter Viereck

Peter Viereck was a historian, social critic, and poet who wrote about the role of Conservatives in America. In the 1950s, Viereck stimulated American intellectuals with interesting ideas on the cultural and political problems of the post-World War II era. He called for increased appreciation of the Western ethical heritage of Christian and Judaic religions and Greco-Roman and European humanism, all of which were threatened by modern commercialism and the mass media. Viereck made a strong case for the relevance of Burkean and Federalist wisdom rooted in Anglo-American freedoms, if directed toward humane governance, the politics of moderation, and the avoidance of the extremes of the Left and Right.

Viereck appeared on the scene after he published an article *But – I'm a Conservative,* in *Atlantic Monthly* (April 1940). The article lays out his evolving philosophy of government and society, which attacked change for its own sake. Viereck lobbied for caution in thinking Communism and Fascism were valid counterweights to Democracy. In those cases, the rule of law became an option rather than a requirement, so

Totalitarianism followed. Fears about Totalitarianism were validated by the tragedy of World War II and the legacy of Socialist failures.

Viereck's most well-known book, *Conservatism Revisited: The Revolt Against Ideology* (1949), delineated his views on the history and role of Conservatism as foundational to the preservation of human society:

> Conservatism is a treasure house, sometimes an infuriatingly dusty one, of generations of accumulative experience, which any ephemeral rebellious generation has a right to discard – at its peril. To vary the metaphor; conservatism is a social and cultural cement, holding together what Western man has built and by that very fact providing a base for orderly change and improvement.[27]

Viereck did not suggest that all history was worth keeping. It is the Conservative's job to maintain history discriminately, even when that history is shameful. Those shameful lessons are as important as positive ones. A sound-thinking Conservative views tradition as a set of ethically acceptable experiences from the past. In times of prosperity, Conservatives must help identify the differences between value and price. That means they must separate value categories like wisdom, from less meaningful categories, like the accumulation of wealth. In times of failure, Conservatives must fight for the rule of law, no matter how

---

[27] Viereck, "Conservatism Revisited."

difficult the crisis. If laws are discarded, anarchy will follow. According to Viereck, mankind can only endure and sustain itself if it is guided by a sense of what is valuable and part of tradition. Society exists to set rules in place that all people must obey. Educational programs must contain some Conservative elements to help create unbreakable ethical beliefs. It is law and tradition that pulled man out of the cave.

Viereck was heavily criticized by the Right and Left for having a weak ideology. The criticism from the Right was based on his incompatibility with the Right's inflexible ideology. The Right claimed he was ideologically wishy-washy and not sufficiently committed to their cause. Today, Viereck's ideas have a sounder footing. Dealing with the current tribal conflict in the United States requires a practical approach to help re-build communications between the Right and Left.

Conservatives are criticized because their process is clumsy, haphazard, and causes pain along the way. Because they are driven by gut instinct, Conservatives rely on traditions as their roadmap. It's important for the Left and the Right to agree on what parts of history should endure as lessons. Such agreement has been elusive because of the historic antagonism between competing ideologies. Today, in this time of tribalism, the problem is worse than ever.

Conservatives are criticized when they use law and tradition to block reform rather than using them to facilitate it. Throughout history, they have helped the peaceful evolution of change in order to avoid revolution. When those in power, via wealth or status, discard their duty to lead, they exploit rather than guide. When government action goes too far and increases the size of the welfare state, it must be reversed. The bloated state steals liberty from the people and doesn't offer the equivalent return.

To prevent majority rule from becoming anarchy, stable societies must use traditional institutions as brakes against the whims of the masses. Traditions must be used to fight against majority rule because a government elected by the majority can make its own rules. A dictatorship can replace an unconservative democracy, either when change is too rapid, or when majority rule dictates policy. At that point, there is no going back.

Socialists pursue a false tradeoff when they place bread above liberty. What good is bread without freedom? Since organization implies the presence of values, accepting those values must be preeminent. Socialists believe it is only possible to achieve the goals of materialism through an idealistic interpretation of life, but human beings have never been willing to subvert themselves to some economic principle. They keep their own counsel and operate instinctively. Dostoevsky described this nicely in his 1864 novella *Notes from the Underground:*

> You gentlemen have taken your register of human advantages from the averages of statistical figures and politico-economic formulas… Shower upon man every earthly blessing, drown him in a sea of happiness, so

that nothing but bubbles of bliss can be seen on the surface... give him economic prosperity such that he should have nothing to do but sleep, eat cake, and busy himself with the continuation of his species and even then, out of shear ingratitude, sheer spite, man would play you some nasty trick. He would even risk his cake desiring the most fatal rubbish the most uneconomically absurdity, simply to introduce into all this good sense his final element, to prove himself as if it were necessary that men are men and not the keys to a piano. The whole work of man seems to be nothing but proving to himself every minute that he is not a piano key.[28]

Those on the Left commonly criticize religious Conservatives for clinging to an obsolete ideology in the time of the rise of the technical economy. They do not understand that religion can be a symbolic experience, as well as a practical one. A vanguard for all that is new, the Left will also bring us pagan Totalitarianism, the lifeless, bleak, soulless equality they admire. By throwing away religion, they abandon their life insurance against disaster. The Conservatives' counter argument is that religion is embedded in the history and the morality of Western society. It endures as a vital component of human relationships through collective moral principles and unifying tenets.

History provides evidence from the past of the civilizing

---

[28] Dostoevsky, "Notes from the Underground."

effects of an advancing morality on barbarians invading groups, towns, cities, and nations from the outside. History identifies today's invaders, but they are coming from the inside. They are individuals who believe the end justifies the means, along with those who choose to ignore the standards of civilized conduct that have endured since they were put into place.

Political Trends

Political demographics are becoming more and more significant in the United States with each passing year. The polarization of the electorate is now translating into a geographical divide. The Left is moving to the big cities, while the Right continues as suburban or rural constituencies. That trend along with immigration is raising the odds that the Democratic Party will have a distinct voter advantage in the coming decades. The percentage of Independents is also increasing over time. That is a good thing; it shows more people reject partisan extremes and want to separate themselves from party bias.

For fundamental reasons, the deck is stacked against Conservatives. First, they waste enormous time on ideological purity, which can only be applied if their candidates are elected. Second, they do not state their case loudly. Conservatives tend to live their lives around traditional social elements (family, church, and community). They are not particularly interested in change, so they are energized to resist change. They are often criticized for absorbing attacks from the other side without responding. This lack of engagement leaves the impression that the opposition's accusations are true. Conservatives must create a greater focus on empathy, which would help deflect the Left's criticisms of Capitalism and what they regard as the uncaring nature of Conservatives.

What the Conservatives have in their favor is the Conservative Gene, upon which a foundational morality has been built within the individual. If you strip away a Conservative ideology and Conservative politics, the gene remains a source of strength. It can carry Conservatives forward through any challenge. Those on the Left do not possess the same toolkit. Their drive for equality and fairness has them seeking a utopian world of equality. When those ideals fail in practice, they have no foundation to use as a replacement.

Points to Remember
1. The history of American Conservatism shows how it became political during the Civil War period and ideological after World War II.

2. The 21st Century elections of Bush, Obama, and Trump have damaged the Conservative ideology, which was already fractured when the new century began.

3. Conservative ideology will continue to move forward, relying on Traditionalist and Libertarian roots, and continue its strong support of Capitalism.

4. Conservatives want to protect Moral Capital, family, community, church, and nation, against the forces that try to destroy them.

5. The most important contribution of Conservatives is to act as a brake against the excesses of the Left. There is nothing inherently wrong with the Lefts' intentions, but when they operate unchecked, tribalism and instability follow.

BIBLIOGRAPHY

Alford, J. R., Funk, C. L., & Hibbing, J. R. "Are political orientations genetically transmitted?" *American Political Science Review* 99, (2005): 153-167.

Allitt, Patrick. *The Conservatives: Ideas and Personalities Throughout American History*. New Haven: Yale University Press, 2009.

Belloni, Frank P, and Beller, Dennis C. The Study of Party Factions as Competitive Political Organizations. *The Western Political Quarterly*, 29, No. 4 (December, 1976): 531-549.

Bohannan, Paul. *Social Anthropology*. New York: Holt, Rinehart and Winston, 1963.

Buckley, William F. *God and Man at Yale*. South Bend, Indiana: Gateway Editions, 1951.

Buckley, William F. *Up from Liberalism*. Mansfield Centre, Connecticut: Martino Publishing, 2016.

Burke, Edmund. *Reflection on the Revolution in France*. Oxford: Oxford University Press, 1790.

231

Burnham, James. *Suicide of the West: An Essay on the Meaning and Destiny of Liberalism*. New York: Encounter Books, 2014.

Campbell, James E. *Making Sense of a Divided America*. Chapter Title: Ideology and Polarization. Book Title: Polarized. Princeton, New Jersey: Princeton University Press, 2016.

Chambers, Whittaker. *Witness*. Washington, D.C: Regnery Publishing, 1952.

Dean, T. *Evolution and Moral Diversity*. The Baltic International Yearbook of Cognition, Logic and Communication. 7. doi:10.4148/biyclc.v7i0.1775, 2012.

Dostoevsky, Fyodor. *Notes from the Underground*. Translated by Constance Garrett. New York: McMillan Company, 1918.

Edwards, Mickey. *American Tribalism*. Chapter in *The Parties Versus the People*. New Haven: Yale University Press, 2012.

Fukuyama, Francis. *The Origins of Political Order, from Pre-human Times to the French Revolution*. New York: Farrar, Straus, and Giroux, 2011.

Fukuyama, Francis. *Political Order and Political Decay, from the Industrial Revolution to the Globalization of Democracy*. New York: Farrar, Straus, and Giroux, 2011.

Helzer, Erik G, and Pizarro, David A. "Dirty Liberals! Reminders of Physical Cleanliness Influence Moral and Political Attitudes." *Psychological Science*, 22, 4 (April, 2011): 517-522.

Goldman, Samuel. *What Is the Future of Conservatism?* Lawliberty.org, (May, 2017).

Goldwater, Barry. *Conscience of a Conservative.* Blacksburg, West Virginia: Wilder Publications, 2009.

Haidt, Jonathan. *The Righteous Mind, Why Good People are divided by Politics and Religion.* New York: Pantheon Books, 2012.

Harvey, David. *A Brief History of Neoliberalism.* Oxford: Oxford University Press, 2005.

Hauser, Marc D. *Moral Minds. How Nature Designed our Universal Sense of Right and Wrong.* New York: Harper Collins, 2006.

Hawkins, Stephen, Yudkin, Daniel, Juan-Torres, Miriam, and Dixon, Tim. "Hidden Tribes: A Study of America's Polarized Landscape." *More in Common,* 2018.

Hayek, Fredrich A. *The Road to Serfdom.* London: University of Chicago Press, 2007.

Hayek, Fredrich A. *Why I am not a Conservative*. The Constitution of Liberty. Chicago: The University of Chicago Press, 1960.

Hogg, Quintin Baron Hailsham of St. Marylebone (1959). *The Conservative Case*. London, Penguin Books.

Horowitz, Irving Louis. "The New Conservatism." *Science & Society*, 20, 1 (Winter, 1956): 1-26.

Hughes, John A., Martin, Peter J., and Sharrock, W.E. *Understanding Classical Sociology: Marx, Weber, Durkheim*. London: Sage Publications, 1995.

Huntington, Samuel P. 1993. "The Clash of Civilizations?" *Foreign Affairs*, 72, No. 3 (Summer, 1993): 22-49

Johnson, Paul. *Modern Times*. The World from the Twenties to the Eighties. New York: Harper and Row, 1983.

Johnson, Paul. *Enemies of Society*. London: Weidenfeld & Nicolson, 1977.

Jost, J. T., Glaser, J., Kruglanski, A. W., & Sulloway, F. 2003b. "Political conservatism as motivated social cognition." *Psychological Bulletin*. 129, (2003): 339-375

Jost, J. T., Nosek, B. A., & Gosling, S. D. "Ideology: Its resurgence in social, personality, and political psychology." *Perspectives on Psychological Science*, 3, (2008): 126-136.

Kanai, R. "Political Orientations are Correlated with Brain Structures in Young Adults." *Current Biology*, 21, 8, (2011): 677-80.

Kimball, Roger. *Tenured Radicals: How Politics has Corrupted our Higher Education.* New York: Harper and Row, 1990.

Kirk, Russell. *The Conservative Mind: From Burke to Eliot.* Washington, D.C: Regnery Publishing, 1953.

Kornhauser, William. *The Politics of Mass Society.* Glencoe, Illinois: The Free Press, 1959.

Krauthammer, Charles. *In the Politically Correct "New History," Victimization is in, Fact are Out.* Pittsburgh Post-Gazette November 7, 1994, B2.

Lincoln, Abraham. *Letter to Joshua Speed.* August 24th, 1855.

Link, Arthur S. American Epoch. *A History of the United States since the 1890s.* New York: Alfred A. Knopf, 1967.

Mt. Pelerin Society. *Statement of Aims*, 1947.

Meyer, Frank S. *What is Conservatism?* Wilmington, Delaware, Intercollegiate Studies Group, 1964.

Mirabeau, Honore Comte de. *Speech*, June 22, 1789.

Murray, Charles. *Coming Apart: The State of White America, 1960-2010*. New York: Crown Forum, 2012.

Nash, George H. *The Conservative Intellectual Movement in America*. Wilmington, Delaware: Intercollegiate Studies Group, 1976.

Nettels, Curtis P. *The Roots of American Civilization. A History of American Colonial Life*. New York: Appleton-Century-Crofts, 1963.

Nice, David C. "Polarization in the American Party System." *Presidential Studies Quarterly*, Vol. 14, No. 1, Campaign '84: The Contest for National Leadership (Winter, 1984), 109-116

Ortega y Gassat, Jose, *Revolt of the Masses*. New York: W.W. Norton & Company, 1994.

Pew Research Center. *Public's Views on Human Evolution*. December 13, 2013.

Pew Research Center. *The landscape of Marriage and Cohabitation in the U.S.* November 6, 2019.

Phillips-Fein, Kim. 2011. "Conservatism: A State of the Field." *The Journal of American History*, Vol. 98, No. 3 (December), pp. 723-743.

Pinker, Steven. *The Blank Slate. The Modern Denial of Human Nature*. New York: Penguin Putnam, 2002.

Povcalnet World Bank. Poverty Head Count 1981-2030. www.ourworldindata.org/extreme poverty.

Putnam, Robert D. *Bowling Alone*. New York: Simon & Schuster. 2000.

Shermer, Elizabeth Tandy. "Collapse or Triumph? The Modern American Conservative Movement at Sixty." *American Studies Journal*, Number 65, (2018).

Service, Elman R. *Primitive Social Organization. An Evolutionary Perspective*. New York: Random House, 1962.

Service, Elman R. *The Origins of the State and Civilization. The Process of Cultural Evolution*. New York: W.W. Norton, 1975.

Shapiro, Ian. *The Moral Foundations of Politics*. New Haven: Yale University Press, 2003.

Shils, Edward. "Special Issue on Tradition and Modernity," *Comparative Studies in Society and History*, Vol. 13, No. 2, (Apr., 1971), 122-159.

Smith, Stephen. *Political Philosophy*. New London: Yale University Press, 2012.

Turiel, Elliot. *The Culture of Morality*. Cambridge: Cambridge University Press, 2002.

Tyrell, R. Emmett. *The Conservative Crack-up*. New York: Simon & Schuster, 1992.

Viereck, Peter. *Conservatism Revisited. The Revolt Against Ideology*. New York: Charles Scribner, 1949.

Weaver, Richard W. 2013. *Ideas Have Consequences*. Chicago, University of Chicago Press, 2013.

Wolfe, Alan. Chapter Title: *The Revolution That Never Was*. Book Title: An Intellectual in Public. Ann Arbor: University of Michigan Press, 2003.

Wunderlin, Clarence E. *The Papers of Robert A. Taft*, Volume 1. Kent, Ohio: Kent State University Press, 1997.

Zelizer, Julian E. Chapter Title: *How Conservatives Learned to Stop Worrying and Love Presidential Power*. Book Subtitle: The Revival of Political History. Book Title: Governing America. Princeton, New Jersey, Princeton University Press, 2012.

Zumbrunnen, John and Gangl, Amy. "Conflict, Fusion, or Coexistence? The Complexity of Contemporary American Conservatism." *Political Behavior*, Vol. 30, No. 2 (Jun 2008), 199-221.

www.ingramcontent.com/pod-product-compliance
Lightning Source LLC
Chambersburg PA
CBHW030240030426
42336CB00009B/191